Peace from Nervous Suffering

Peace from Nervous Suffering

by Dr. Claire Weekes,
M.B., D.Sc., M.R.A.C.P.

*Consultant Physician to the Rachel Forster Hospital,
Sydney, Australia*

HAWTHORN BOOKS, INC.
Publishers
New York

Library of Congress Catalog Card Number: 70-169865

ISBN: 0-8015-5804-2

11 12

Dedicated as a token of esteem to the many
whose courage has helped to make this book

Preface

Peace from Nervous Suffering is offered as treatment for nervous illness, not merely as reading. The nervously disturbed person is often so tired and confused he finds concentrating and remembering difficult; therefore I have written this book with as much emphasis—repetition, even italics—as I thought helpful.

In my earlier book, *Hope and Help for Your Nerves,* I talked about the commonest kind of nervous illness—the anxiety state (often called nervous breakdown). In the present book, whereas I offer additional help to those suffering from the anxiety state in general, I offer special help to those whose illnesses are dominated by a particular fear—agoraphobia. Agoraphobia is fear of leaving the safety of home, of traveling alone—even as far as the corner of the street to post a letter. It includes fear of wide-open spaces as well as fear of being in crowded places—a school hall, a restaurant, even church.

To my knowledge, this is the first book written by a doctor that directly addresses sufferers from this crippling illness. Indeed, other than treatises on agoraphobia written for medical journals, or mention of it in books on fears and phobias, this is the first book dealing mainly with agoraphobia itself. It is estimated that more than a million people suffer from agoraphobia in the United States alone. The number is probably far greater, as so many sufferers do not seek help for their illness; many even hide it. Although so widespread, agoraphobia has only recently been recognized by doctors generally. It is arousing much interest in America and England today, however, and the future promises improved understanding and treatment for many people who, so far, have thought themselves alone, unnoticed, even unique, in their illness.

During 1968–1970 I wrote eight quarterly journals that reached 1,300 sufferers from nervous illness—the majority with agoraphobia—in the British Isles, the United States of America, Canada, Australia, New Zealand, South Africa, Hong Kong, India, and recently Japan. These journals are already well known, but this is their first printing in book form in America.

C. W.
London

Contents

Peace from Nervous Suffering

1

Sensitization: The Simple Cause of So Much Nervous Illness

If nervous suffering has led you to this book, you may have picked it up with both hope and doubt. Possibly you have tried so hard to recover in the past and have —as you think—let yourself down so often that you may hesitate to trust yourself to try again. Perhaps you have been ill so long you suspect you are beyond help. Small wonder doubt is mixed with hope. And yet, I assure you, however often you may have failed in the past, however long you may have suffered, you can recover.

Perhaps, like so many of my nervously ill patients, you have no personality defect making or keeping you ill; indeed, you may have no particular problem except finding the way to recovery. Many of my patients were happy in their home life and at work until they became ill. They then became afraid of the state they were in, *of the way they felt*—not only of what was happening at the time but also of what they feared might yet be in store. Without realizing it, their nerves had tricked them, duped them.

TRICKS YOUR NERVES PLAY

Through the years I have seen every shade of every trick my patients' nerves have played upon them; I saw how easily, how unwittingly, many were led into nervous illness, and because of this I want to open your eyes to the way your nerves could now be tricking you.

We should know there are three special pitfalls that can lead to nervous illness, and above all we should know how to cope with them. The three pitfalls are *sensitization, bewilderment,* and *fear.* Sensitization is a state in which nerves are conditioned to react to stress in an exaggerated way; that is, they bring unusually intense feelings when under stress, and at times with alarming swiftness.

There is no mystery about sensitization. Most of us have surely felt it in a mild way when we have been working under pressure and our nerves have become ale. .ed to respond too quickly, too acutely, to situations that would, at other times, leave us unmoved. When mildly sensitized, we may be irritated by those near us, impatient when driving home in heavy traffic or waiting for the evening bus. We continue working, driving, traveling, however, and these feelings will gradually pass.

On the other hand, severe sensitization can be upsetting indeed. Besides feeling painfully edgy and agitated, a severely sensitized person may feel his heart constantly beating quickly, "missing" beats, or thumping; he may have recurring attacks of palpitations; he may feel his stomach churn—especially on waking in the morning or after an afternoon nap. His hands may tremble and sweat. He may have difficulty expanding his chest to take in a deep breath and may—in the words of one woman—gasp and gulp for air. He may complain of a lump in his throat which seems to interfere with swallowing solid food, or he may have weak turns. He may suffer from headaches

—a feeling of weight pressing on top of his head, of an "iron band" around it; giddiness; or a sensation of lurching, swaying, or of being pulled to one side while walking.

Most alarming of all, panic may come so easily and swiftly that the slightest shock may bring it: perhaps no more than the unexpected sound of a slamming door. More bewildering still, panic may come for no apparent reason. Although these are no more than the usual symptoms of stress exaggerated by sensitization, the sufferer rarely recognizes them as stress symptoms. He thinks they are unique to him, that no one could have possibly suffered this way before.

SUDDEN SENSITIZATION

One need not be a special type to become sensitized. Quite severe sensitization can be suddenly and unexpectedly thrust upon any one of us at any time. It may follow the stress of a physical shock to our nerves, such as an exhausting surgical operation, a heavy hemorrhage, a difficult confinement, an accident, and so on.

For example, when severe sensitization follows a surgical operation, the simplest postoperative routine—such as a finger prick for a blood count or the dressing of a wound—can almost reduce its victim to tears. Any frustration, perhaps no more than waiting for the doctor to arrive, may bring intense agitation and make nerves feel so taut that a sudden noise jars painfully. Also, panic can follow the slightest anxious thought: *hence the necessity to understand sensitization and know how to cope with it.*

A retired nursing sister who had been in charge of a surgical ward for years said recently, "If I had known more about sensitization when I was nursing, how much more understanding I could have given my patients." At that time she was sensitized herself.

GRADUAL SENSITIZATION

Of course, severe sensitization can come about more slowly. It may gradually accompany continuous domestic stress, too strenuous dieting, a debilitating illness—anything that puts nerves under stress for a prolonged time. The stress need not necessarily be unhappy. An actor constantly alert to give his best performance may become quite sensitized, especially if he neglects sleep and food.

THE PATTERN IS LIMITED

Since the symptoms of sensitization are the symptoms of stress, they conform to the usual pattern of stress symptoms. This pattern is set, limited, because nerves under stress always release the same chemicals, which act on the same organs and always produce the same results. It comforts a sufferer to learn that the pattern of his suffering is limited and that he has probably already experienced the severest symptoms his nerves can bring. I have seen this information alone cure some people. Because their body had brought them so many surprises in the past and had, as they thought, let them down so badly, they were constantly worried about what further surprises the future might yet hold.

HOW NERVES NORMALLY FUNCTION

When we say someone is suffering from nerves, we do not only means nerves are stimulated to bring certain symptoms, but we also imply that nerves have "gone wrong" and are somehow at fault. Actually they are responding faithfully and physiologically to the messages sent to them. To be cured one should understand this, and to do so it is essential to know how nerves normally function. Although I described this in detail in my earlier book,

Hope and Help for Your Nerves, it is necessary to repeat the description at least briefly here.

Our nervous system consists of two parts: voluntary and involuntary. By means of our voluntary nerves we move our muscles (hence our body) more or less as we wish. These nerves obey our direct command, so we call them voluntary. The involuntary nerves help our glands control the functioning of our organs—heart, lungs, bowels, and so on. Unlike the voluntary nerves, we have (with a few exceptions) no direct control over them—hence the term "involuntary."

The involuntary nerves themselves consist of two divisions, sympathetic and parasympathetic. In a peaceful body these two hold each other in check. If we are emotional, however—afraid, angry, excited, agitated—the sympathetic usually dominates the parasympathetic, and we are aware of certain organs functioning: We may feel our heart race and pound, we may breathe quickly, our hands may sweat, and so on. Sympathetic nerves produce these reactions mainly by means of a chemical called adrenaline, which is released at the nerve endings in the organs concerned.

Normally when afraid, we accept our racing heart, rapid breathing, even the spasm of fear in our "middle," because we know that when the cause of the fear goes, these reactions will also pass. Our feelings calm because we no longer think fearfully. Changing mood (attitude) is the only conscious control other than medication we have over our symptoms of stress. I emphasize this because understanding it is of paramount importance in understanding recovery from so much nervous illness.

BEWILDERMENT AND FEAR

Now I come to a point I wish to highlight: *The symptoms of much nervous illness are no more than the*

symptoms of stress exaggerated by severe sensitization.
One might well ask, What is the difference between severe
sensitization and nervous illness? When do we say someone is merely sensitized and when nervously ill? And how
does he pass from sensitization to nervous illness?

We say a person is nervously ill when sensitization
upsets him so much that it interferes with his way of life.
Someone who has never been sensitized might well then
ask, What keeps a person sensitized long enough for this
to happen? And this is a good question, because it brings
us face to face with those other two culprits previously
mentioned, *bewilderment* and *fear*.

Bewilderment and fear keep sensitization alive. Bewilderment acts by placing a sensitized person constantly under
the strain of asking himself, What is wrong with me?
Why am I like this? The more he struggles to be the person
he was, the more exasperation, the more tension, and
consequently the more stress he adds. His failure to find
a way out of this maze makes him feel incapable of coping
with any future course his illness might take, and he
vaguely sees himself being "taken away somewhere."

While he feels in his bewilderment that he cannot direct
his thoughts and actions adequately, he stands especially
vulnerable to, and defenseless before, fear, which can
overwhelm him before he has time to reason with it. It is
the stress of bewilderment and fear continually being
added to the stress of the original sensitization that keeps
this sensitization alive and keeps its symptoms so severe.
The sensitized person puts himself in a cycle of fear-
adrenaline-fear. In other words, his fear of the state he
is in produces the adrenaline and other stress hormones,
which continue to excite his nerves to produce the very
symptoms he fears. The fear-adrenaline-fear cycle is also
called an anxiety state.

So many of the people who have come to me for help
have had no particular problem or no cause in their sub-

conscious either creating their illnesses or keeping them ill. Their main difficulties were finding the way to recovery and trying to meet responsibilities that because of illness seemed beyond them. They had been tricked into illness by those three bogeys, sensitization, bewilderment, and fear.

THE HABIT OF FEAR

In my opinion, too much time is spent and too much suffering is caused today by unnecessary searching for deep-seated causes of nervous illness when so often none exist. It is not enough to be told that such and such happened when one was young and that this is why one is nervous now. Whatever may have originally caused the illness —and in my experience it is by no means as often a childhood cause as is commonly believed—*present sensitization remains.* The habit of fear is the important thing now. *This must be cured.*

A woman from America wrote:

> I saw a doctor four years ago, but out of sheer frustration, I quit. He did nothing but continually rehash the past. All I seemed to hear was that my mother left me to the maids and my father didn't love me either. I have been told over and over again that lack of love caused my acute phobias, but never how to handle the fears themselves, especially fear of leaving home alone. I have repeatedly asked for help to deal with today, with the acute and constant fears and awful physical feelings I have. It seems all I've been given to live with is "but if" and "if only."

This is not an isolated cry. It comes from many. Until the importance of straightforward sensitization is recognized as a possible cause of nervous illness, our present rate of cure will not improve as much as it otherwise would. I stress again that so much nervous illness has no deep-seated cause and is no more than severe sensitization—perhaps accidentally acquired—kept alive by bewilderment and fear.

The nervously ill person is forever questioning not only himself but also others. Too often the answers are so unsatisfactory that he loses hope of ever finding the explanation he craves, especially if he has been ill for long. Should you be suffering like this, you need a full explanation of what is happening to you. You also need a program for recovery, and that is what I offer in this book.

2

Fear of Leaving the Safety of Home (Agoraphobia)

"Agoraphobia" literally means "fear of the marketplace," an abnormal fear of being in open or public places. In medical practice it refers to fear of leaving the safety of home either alone or in company. It is a much more crippling fear than claustrophobia—fear of enclosed places.

Until recently few people had heard of agoraphobia; even some doctors did not know the term. Four years ago, I accompanied a patient to see an ophthalmic surgeon of many years' experience. I explained to him that the patient suffered with agoraphobia and mentioned the possible temporary effect of the tension on her vision. He listened politely, but when we were leaving, said, "I don't believe in this illness you call agoraphobia. It doesn't exist!" Since then there has been much publicity in England about the housebound housewife (suffering from agoraphobia) in newspapers and magazines and on radio and television; I doubt if that surgeon would say the same today.

It is possible this particular phase of nervous illness received so little attention in the past because an agoraphobic person often feels too self-conscious about his fears to discuss them even with a doctor. It is not easy for a woman to confess, especially to a man who she thinks may be unbelieving (as was that surgeon), that she is afraid to go to the supermarket alone and must either take a child with her for protection or send the child to do the shopping. It is just as difficult for a man to explain that he prefers to stay in a subordinate position at work because he cannot face taking a higher position that would mean traveling from city to city when he finds it so difficult to leave his own town.

This fear is not only difficult to explain to others but also difficult for the sufferers to understand themselves. Most of them used not to be like this, and they look back now in amazement at how freely they could once travel. This is why they think their illness is peculiar, something to be ashamed of, and why they are so surprised when they learn that many sensible, even notable, people suffer just as they do. After I have spoken about agoraphobia on radio or television, the studio switchboard is frequently jammed with incoming calls from people who have heard themselves and their fears described for the first time. Acknowledgment that the origin of their illness could be simple, the detailed description of how they feel, and especially recognition of the importance of their fear of fear are the reassurance they had been wanting for so long and had despaired of finding.

THE SAFETY ZONE

The sufferer from agoraphobia does not really think some particular place holds a special danger for him and that something there will harm him. He is afraid of how he will *react* when in a certain situation. He has become so sensitively aware of what happens within himself at the slightest stress—of how he panics, feels weak and giddy, and so on—that he lives in fear that these feelings will arise in places where he thinks he will be unable to cope with them and where he may consequently make a fool of himself in front of others. So the housewife clings to her home and the executive to his own hometown. They cling to their safety zone. This is why the nervous person sits at the back of the school meeting, on the aisle at the cinema, near the door in the restaurant—so that he can slip out quickly and unnoticed if he feels one of his turns coming. He specially dreads being in an airplane, a train, any vehicle he cannot stop and leave at will.

The interest aroused in agoraphobia today has led to surveys being made—principally in the British Isles—of groups of agoraphobic sufferers with special regard to cause and results of treatment. In my experience the cause in most people has been easy to find. Often agoraphobia begins with an unexpected attack of palpitations, giddiness, or perhaps weakness—a feeling of collapse—while the person is out. Frequently it has followed a sudden, unaccountable attack of severe panic. The basic cause of these attacks has usually been fatigue or some other form of stress, following a variety of experiences—difficult confinement, debilitating illness, and so on. Occasionally there is no obvious reason, and happily I have rarely found disclosing an original cause of agoraphobia essential for cure.

It will surely be appreciated how easily a housewife can be frightened by an attack of palpitations and then become afraid to venture far from home for fear of having a "heart attack" while out. Anything unusual to do with the heart is upsetting, and a sudden attack of palpitations can be alarming, especially if it comes when a person is alone and away from home. If the sufferer has more than one attack, she may be convinced there is something radically wrong with her heart. If she goes immediately to a doctor who reassures her that the trouble is "only nerves" and helps her to become reconciled to having an occasional attack until her health improves, all may be well. If she does not accept his reassurance, however, she may be constantly worried about her heart, especially if she has further attacks, and may be especially afraid the palpitations will come when she is where she cannot get help readily. Hence she develops a growing reluctance to move far from the house.

A lecturer, afraid of having an attack of palpitations while speaking before an audience, gradually lost so much confidence he would not speak unless his wife was present. This is not as childish as it sounds because he was most likely to have an attack when apprehensive, and he was most apprehensive while lecturing. His wife's presence gave him a feeling of support which allayed his fear.

If a housewife, afraid of a heart attack (as she wrongly diagnoses palpitations) or of a weak turn or of panic, manages to walk as far as the supermarket, how natural, when faced with waiting in the check-out line, for her to be suddenly smitten with the thought, "What if I had a turn now?" Fear and tension can quickly agitate a sensitized person, and the feeling of vulnerability that comes with agitation will soon convince her that her symptoms could build up into one of her spells. This results in her eventual decision to avoid the supermarket or to find someone to shop with her.

No Respecter of Sex

More women than men suffer from agoraphobia. A woman's life at home lends itself to the development of agoraphobia. There are agoraphobic men, however, and they, as mentioned earlier, whereas accustomed to leaving the house daily, usually show their illness by refusing to leave their own town. Many a deputy chief would be chief today were he not afraid of the traveling involved in seniority. I call this the citybound-executive syndrome.

Symptoms are no respecter of sex. A nervously ill man complains of the same symptoms as a nervous woman: palpitations, weak turns, giddiness, trembling, panic. These symptoms are not as "feminine" as one has been conditioned to think. They are the symptoms of stress and therefore experienced by men and women alike.

Weak spells are just as upsetting as palpitations. If the sufferer panics while out because of having a weak spell, she may feel so exhausted that she is sure she can go no further and must return home. How quickly those weak legs move when once headed toward the house, though. If instead of returning home, she tries to fight her way forward or by grim determination she stays in the supermarket (or any other place), mounting tension may so stiffen her muscles that she may feel locked in tension and stand "paralyzed," holding onto the nearest support, unable—so she thinks—to move. She especially dreads a big emporium, where the crowd, heat, noise, and the absence of a place to sit seem to invite that faint feeling.

THE PAVEMENT SEEMS TO HEAVE

Giddiness is especially dreaded, and the sufferer is not so easily convinced that such a disturbing physical sensation can be caused by nerves. One woman said, "When I am overtired, I get giddy, and I've still got to convince myself the giddiness is only fatigue because when I am tired, it's hard to convince myself of anything." The thought of a brain tumor may haunt a woman who suffers from giddiness. Even if finally persuaded that nerves are the culprit, she finds walking down the street difficult, for the pavement seems to heave, the shops to topple. Nor is it easy to stay in the supermarket while the goods on the shelves seem to sway. In addition, tension may affect her sight, so that from time to time objects appear blurred and the distant view is covered with a shimmering haze.

Surely it is not difficult to understand how this woman, having these experiences, gradually comes to prefer to stay at home or take someone—even a child—to shop with her. If she takes a child, it may not be long before she becomes afraid the child will notice her peculiarities and see her "like this," so she may postpone shopping until her husband can accompany her.

EXPOSING A CHILDHOOD CAUSE IS RARELY HELPFUL

An important part of treatment lies in showing a sensitized woman or man how to cope with the exaggerated symptoms of stress, particularly panic, so that they gradually desensitize themselves and, if agoraphobic, are no longer afraid to be alone, travel alone, be surrounded by people, or take the strain of waiting in line. As I said earlier, finding a childhood cause for present illness may be interesting, but it rarely helps cope with the present condition, especially if the sufferer has been ill a long time.

A happily married woman who had suffered for years from agoraphobia was told by an analyst that her reluctance to go out alone was based on a subconscious fear of becoming a prostitute; however, this woman had begun to have faint spells while driving a munitions wagon during World War II and naturally lost confidence in driving alone. The cause of her spells was probably fatigue. She had certainly not had enough rest or food. It was obvious from her history that the attacks she had later, during the years that followed, were induced by memory and fear of having a turn where she could not get help or where one would be humiliating or dangerous—in a crowd, driving a car, and so on. The orbit within which she could move gradually became so restricted that she could finally drive only a few miles from home, could not enter a big store alone, and could go on holiday only if accompanied there and back by a doctor. Naturally, she and the family took few holidays. She was finally taught by explanation and encouragement how to cope with her fears. Part of her story, written by her, is in Journal 8.

So Confident on Monday, So Defeated on Tuesday

So much depends on a doctor's ability to explain why, when the patient is feeling better, a setback can come for no special reason—at least none that the patient can see— and be so immediately devastating, as if no progress had been made; why symptoms thought forgotten can return so acutely after months of absence; why all the symptoms can appear, one after the other; why panic can come "out of the blue"; why such demoralizing exhaustion can so rapidly follow stress; why, despite the right attitude, sensitization may linger on for such an unexpectedly long time; why, when the patient returns home after being especially successful, it may seem as if no success had been achieved and why going out the next day can be as difficult as ever. The "whys" seem countless. Unless a doctor has the necessary understanding, his advice may only induce pessimism. An agoraphobic woman wrote about herself and her fellow sufferers, "If unmarried, we may be patted on the back and told we will be better when married; if married, that having a child will fix us; if middle-aged, that it's 'the change'!"

To Be Afraid Is So Human

During interviews on radio and television I have been surprised at the intensity with which some of my colleagues have defended their belief that the anxiety state, including agoraphobia, is due either to some deep-seated cause, often thought to be subconscious, or to some character inadequacy, and that the illness can be cured only if these causes are found and treated. Severe sensitization, however, as already pointed out, can come to any one of us, at any time. To be bewildered by, and afraid of, its acute and baffling symptoms is so human, so natural, that it is difficult to understand why the many people who respond this way should be thought inadequate and different or why finding some deep-seated cause should be thought essential. Sudden severe sensitization can be so shocking that confidence can be quickly shattered, and one does not have to be a dependent type—as I have sometimes heard these sufferers described—to be so affected. If some nervously ill doctors can, with their medical training, fail to understand sensitization or know how to cope with its effects on themselves (and I have seen this), why should a layman be expected *as a matter of course* to be wise enough to do so and to be philosophical about it in the bargain?

Fear is one of the strongest, most disagreeable emotions we know; is it so inconceivable one could be afraid of it for its own sake? Must there always be a cause for fear other than fear of fear? Why cannot fear of fear, when it flashes almost electrically—as it does in a sensitized person—be a cause in itself? It is, you know.

Far from being dependent types, many nervously ill people, although unable to understand what is happening, show great courage and independence fighting their fears, often with little help or sympathy from their family. One woman telephoned recently and said, "Could I possibly have a copy of the journals by the weekend? My husband has said at last that he will read them!" Another woman said, "My husband is much kinder now he knows men suffer this way as well as women!"

A teacher, and intelligent woman, would not remain in a shop unless she clasped in her hand a toy car to remind her of her own car parked nearby, should she feel forced to leave in a hurry. When I mention this woman, listeners are often amused. It is because of such anticipated ridicule that sufferers from agoraphobia are frequently reluctant to confess it, even to their family and friends. Also, whereas a husband may begin by sympathizing with his wife, he may eventually become irritated, critical, and finally desperate at the inconveniences the illness brings. And yet the wife will struggle on heroically, understanding these difficulties only too well and feeling desperately guilty because of them.

PLANS ARE MADE, BROKEN, REMADE, REBROKEN

Contemplating taking an agoraphobic wife on vacation is especially frustrating and exhausting. One minute she says she will go, the next that she cannot make it; so plans are made, broken, remade, rebroken. Reservations are made and canceled several times, with many a deposit forfeited in the meantime. No small part of a husband's frustration lies in his swinging from optimism at some apparent improvement in his wife's condition to disappointment when she slips into a setback, usually for no reason that makes sense to him.

INABILITY TO FEEL LOVE

The wife also has her share of frustration, especially if, because of weariness or lack of interest, her husband fails to give the cooperation she craves. She feels this acutely because frustration, like so many of her emotions, is exaggerated by sensitization. She may think he is wittingly uncooperative, and in a moment of despair, thinks she hates him. Indeed, she is sometimes bewildered by the depth of her antipathy and resentment. Although she knows the old love must be there, she cannot *feel* it. She thinks in confusion, "What is reality, my present dislike or my old love?" She is especially frightened because she feels the dislike so convincingly. One wife wrote, "It is as if I am just about to see through a mist of unreality but never quite make it. I don't know if I really love my husband, because I see him now as another person, not the man I married."

Another woman said, "D., who used to be such a marvelous help, has reached the stage of 'do it yourself,' and I don't get much help from him now. If I have a spell during the night, his pat solution to the whole thing is, 'Roll over and go to sleep!' Doesn't he know by now that if I could roll over and sleep, I would?"

Here again, understanding that inability to feel love is a usual but temporary result of emotional exhaustion helps cheer the sufferer and ease bewilderment and guilt. One should not sigh too deeply for a family's understanding nor pity oneself and think, "If only they knew!" Very few families "know," and most sufferers follow the same lonely road hedged by misunderstanding. Waste no strength on self-pity. It is an expensive emotion; it robs you of the will to go forward and never cured anyone.

Also, do not be too upset if you are told you could recover if you really wanted to. Be consoled. I have rarely met the nervously ill man or woman who had no wish to recover. He or she may have failed so often in their attempt that their spirit seems dead. It usually smolders on, however, ready to rise again for another valiant, if misdirected, effort. Let there be no misunderstanding about this: The vast majority of my nervously ill patients (and I do not use the word "vast" lightly) yearn to recover. Of course, there is the occasional work-dodger who prefers to retreat into illness rather than face the responsibilities of ordinary living, but in my practice these have been rare.

"AM I TRYING TO ESCAPE FROM SOMETHING, DOCTOR?"

Some people ask anxiously, "Am I really trying to escape from something, Doctor? My last doctor said so;

but what am I trying to escape from?" This inquiry often comes from women who want desperately to be shown how to recover. If the husband believes his wife is trying to escape into illness to gain his attention, her desperation is pitiable. Any sensible person would want to escape from, not into, an anxiety state—especially agoraphobia—and the majority of my nervously ill patients have been sensible. They have proved this by the lives they have led after recovery.

During the last two years I have written a quarterly journal for 1,300 sufferers from an anxiety state in many different countries. Most of them had agoraphobia as part of their illness. Had I not been convinced that these people wanted to and could be cured, even by the remote control of journals alone (for I have not seen these people), I would not have spent so much time writing and distributing the journals.

3

Cure of Physical Nervous Symptoms

Solving a problem that originally caused nervous illness does not necessarily cure the illness. To recover, the sufferer may still have to learn how to cope with a habit of easily induced physical nervous symptoms such as panic, palpitations, weakness, and so on. He may also have to cope with certain upsetting and bewildering nervous experiences that have very often arisen from his physical nervous symptoms, experiences such as suggestibility, loss of confidence, feelings of unreality and personality disintegration, and obsession.

However exacting this program may seem, cure depends on four simple rules:

Face; do not run away.
Accept; do not fight.
Float past; do not arrest and listen in.
Let time pass; do not be impatient with time.

When you read these instructions, you may think, "That is too simple. It will take something more drastic than that to cure me!" You will need to study these rules carefully, however, and may need to read the instructions in this book many times before you will grasp their full meaning and know how to apply them successfully. Indeed, it is enlightening to see how many people become deeply sunken in their illnesses *by doing the exact opposite.*

For example, the nervously ill person usually notices each new symptom in alarm, listens in in apprehension, and yet at the same time is afraid to examine it too closely for fear this will make it worse. So he agitatedly seeks occupation to try to force forgetfulness. *This is running away, not facing.*

He may try to cope with the unwelcome feelings by tensing himself against them, thinking, "I must not let this get the better of me!" *He is fighting, not accepting and floating.*

He also keeps looking backward and worrying because so much time has passed and he is not cured—as if there is an evil spirit that could be exorcised if only he or the doctor knew how to do it. *He is impatient with time, is not willing to let time pass.*

Need we be impressed if he thinks it will take something more drastic than facing, accepting and floating, and letting time pass to cure him? I don't think so.

The physical nervous symptoms discussed in this chapter are those that most often deter the nervously ill person from venturing out alone: panic (above all); attacks of palpitation; fairly constantly quickly beating heart; "missed" heartbeats; giddiness; weak turns; a feeling of inability to take a deep breath, including a fear of suffocation; fear of vomiting before others; a feeling of a "lump in the throat," usually accompanied by difficulty in swallowing solid food (especially embarrassing when dining out); trembling hands; deep blushing. A sufferer may have only some

of these symptoms; very few have them all. The most
common nervous experiences (discussed in the next
chapter) are: indecisiveness, suggestibility, loss of confidence, feelings of unreality, feelings of personality disintegration, that dreaded early-morning feeling, strange
thoughts, obsession, and depression.

These symptoms and experiences may be found in any
anxiety state, of which fear of leaving the safety of home
or one's hometown (agoraphobia) may or may not be a
part. So if you are nervously ill but can move freely from
home, you will still find most of your distressing symptoms
and experiences explained and treated here.

PANIC

Understanding the anxiety state based primarily on *fear of
the symptoms of fear* (the kind I have found so prevalent
in my medical practice and the kind I am concentrating on in this book) depends fundamentally on understanding panic and learning how to cope with it because
without the recurring lash of panic, nerves would calm,
and the other physical nervous symptoms (palpitations,
weakness, giddiness, and so on), even upsetting nervous
experiences (loss of confidence, feelings of unreality, and
so on), would be less intense. Panic is particularly domi-
nating in agoraphobia, and this is why I begin discussing
the cure of agoraphobia by first discussing panic. To avoid
panicking while out an agoraphobic woman may arrange
special props. Some push a baby carriage, others lead a dog
on a leash, some wear dark glasses. Many prefer to go out
at night or in the rain because they feel less conspicuous
and expect to meet fewer people. Agoraphobic men also
arrange props. If forced to travel to a new town, they will
immediately locate a doctor or hospital "just in case"!

Such subterfuge gives a certain protection and support,
and the sufferer may eventually gain enough courage to

venture farther and farther from home. The woman (or man) who recovers in this way does not fully understand how she is recovering, however, so there may be that constant menacing thought "What if it were to come back?" Since *it* is fear—stress itself—as long as she is afraid of *it* returning, it is already on its way; even while she is out, she is still keeping the home fires burning.

Also, props have a habit of giving way. The surest path to permanent recovery is to know how to face, and truly accept, fear and not placate it with subterfuge. How simple this sounds; how difficult it can be, and how much support and encouragement the sufferer rightly feels he or she needs while carrying out this apparently simple task.

AT THE MERCY OF SOME "THING"

One of the keys to understanding sensitization lies in realizing that for a sensitized person simply thinking of panic may bring it, or that panic may seem to come unbidden. This is why the sufferer often feels caught in a trap. He will say, "The panic comes so quickly I can't do anything about it." This is why he watches constantly—to leave a way open for quick retreat—and why eventually going out alone or leaving the hometown, with the threat of panic "around the corner," may become too frightening to be contemplated.

It helps in understanding such fear if I compare our automatic nerves with the trigger of a gun. A rusty trigger is stiff to pull; when well oiled, well used, it responds more readily to the touch. The "nerve trigger" of the woman wearing dark glasses and valiantly pushing a perambulator before her is so well used that it fires off (and "fire" is a good word) at even the mere sight of a neighbor to whom she may have to stop and speak. This is especially upsetting because *she used not to feel this way.* Of course not; when she was not sensitized, an inquisitive neighbor's approach meant at most only annoyance, never this flashing fear.

REDUCING PANIC TO NORMAL INTENSITY

Cure lies in developing such insulation to panic that it comes neither so readily nor so acutely. In other words, cure lies in reducing panic to normal frequency and intensity. To do this the nervous person must understand that when he panics, he feels not one fear, as he supposes, but *two separate* fears. In my earlier book I called these the *first* and *second* fears.

The importance of recognizing these two separate fears cannot be overestimated, so I will incorporate here part of the explanation given in that earlier book. I pointed out that although the sensitized person may have no control over the *first* fear, with understanding and practice he can learn how to control the *second* fear. It is this *second* fear that is keeping the *first* alive, keeping him sensitized and nervously ill.

FIRST FEAR

Each of us experiences *first* fear from time to time. It is the fear that comes almost reflexly in response to danger. It is normal in intensity; we understand it and accept it because we know that when the danger passes, the fear will also pass. The flash of *first* fear that comes to a sensitized person in response to danger can be so electric in its swiftness, so out of proportion to the danger causing it, that he cannot readily dismiss it. Indeed, he usually recoils from it, *and as he recoils he adds a second flash of fear. He adds fear of the first fear.* Indeed, he may be much more concerned with the physical feeling of panic than with the original danger. And because that old bogey sensitization prolongs the first flash, the second flash may seem to join it. *This is why the two fears feel as one.*

A flash of *first* fear can come in response to a thought only vaguely understood or to some mildly unpleasant memory, or, as mentioned earlier, it may seem to come unbidden. Can you see how easily victimized a sensitized person can be by *first* fear? All the symptoms of stress— the pounding heart, churning stomach, trembling body, and so on—can be called *first* fear because they too seem to come unbidden, like the flash of panic that comes in response to danger; and to these symptoms the nervously ill person certainly adds much *second* fear.

SECOND FEAR

Pages could be filled with examples of *second* fear, and I doubt if there would be one that some of you have not known at some time. Recognizing *second* fear is easier when we realize it can be prefixed by "Oh, my goodness!" and "What if . . .?" "Oh, my goodness, it took three capsules to get me to sleep last night! What if three don't work tonight?" "What if I get worse, not better?" So many "oh, my goodnesses," so many "what ifs," make up *second* fear. You probably know them all.

The nervously ill person, hemmed in at the school meeting, at church, at the movies, in a restaurant, has but to feel trapped to flash *first* fear, to which he immediately adds *second* fear, as he thinks, "Oh, my goodness, here it is again! I can't stand it. I'll make a fool of myself in front of all these people! Let me out of here! Quickly! Quickly! Quickly!" With each "quickly" he becomes more and more tense, and as the tension mounts, naturally the panic mounts, until he wonders how much longer he can hold on without "cracking." So he takes an even tighter grip on himself and builds up even more tension as the moments pass.

Mounting tension is alarming and exhausting. It is difficult to hold tensely onto oneself for a few minutes, and yet at the school meeting, in church, nervously ill people try to hold tensely onto themselves for an hour or more. Small wonder the panic grows until they are terrified of what crisis it may bring. They are sure there must be a crisis in which "something terrible" will happen, and they vaguely see themselves "collapsing." They are never sure what this "something terrible" might be but feel it hovering menacingly in the background. They can be reassured. There is a limit to the intensity of a spasm of panic even a sensitized body can produce, and they have probably experienced it already. They do not realize this, however, because their imaginations are working overtime.

Their Minds Go Numb

Their fear is so acute and their imaginations so active that at the peak of panic they feel that their minds go numb, that they can neither think nor act clearly. This is why keeping a way open for quick retreat—sitting near the exit—seems so imperative. Nervously ill people do not understand that it is the fears they add themselves, the succession of *second* fears, that may finally drive them to find refuge outside the building.

And when outside, they will probably feel relieved, breathe freely for a while; but as soon as they face the fact that they failed once more, they despair because they think they will never, never be able to sit through another such function. They gave themselves an impossible task; they went through every moment heroically, *but they did it the wrong way.*

If you sometimes seek refuge outside, ask yourself why you can gradually relax when outside yet cannot do so while inside. You will say, "As soon as I am outside, I feel different." The truth is that as soon as you are outside, you think differently, so of course you feel better.

He Always Manages to Say, "Excuse Me, Please!"

When you are sensitized, feeling follows thought so swiftly and intensely that you may be afraid to think while sitting at the school function for fear of what you might think and for fear of what you will then feel. But you do think, don't you? A very vivid imagination is well at work, and sometimes you can almost see yourself becoming hysterical and being led outside. Yet I have never seen or heard of a nervously ill person becoming hysterical at a function. When he, or she, decides he cannot stand another minute and leaves the hall, he always manages to say, "Excuse me, please!" to the person beside him.

Exactly what does happen outside the building that makes outside so much more bearable than inside? If you are the person in this situation, you probably think, "Thank goodness, nothing can happen now!" and you release that tense hold on yourself. First you let it go in thought, and this eases the tense physical hold. If you could do the same inside the building, your problem would be solved. It would, you know. It may seem more complicated than this to you, but it isn't. And yet what is so simple to say is not so simple to do.

First Fear Must Always Die Down

How are you to cope with that feeling of panic, those frightening thoughts, that agitation, when you are inside the school hall? You cope by practicing seeing panic through, even seeing agitation through, with as much acceptance as you can muster. It is all those "oh, my goodnesses," all those "what ifs," that build up into what you call a spell, a crisis. Try to understand that your body is not a machine, that it has a limited capacity to produce adrenaline, that therefore *first* fear can come only in a wave and must always die down *if you but wait* and do not fall into the trap of stoking your fires with more and more *second* fear and so more and more adrenaline. If you remain seated and relax to the best of your ability—even allow your body to slump in the chair—and are prepared to let the panic flash, let it do its very worst without withdrawing tensely from it, *there will be no mounting panic*. Your sensitized body may continue to flash fear from time to time, *but the panic will not mount,* and at least you will be able to see the function through.

Must you let these physical feelings hold such terror? Must you let them, horrible though they may be, spoil your life when the way to calm them is within your own power? Think about this, and understand that *you are bluffed by physical feelings* of no great medical significance. This realization alone has cured some people. If you are prepared to practice seeing panic through, this acceptance, shaky as it may be at first, will bring some peace—enough to lessen the flow of adrenaline and so begin desensitization. It is bombardment by *second* fear, day after day, month after month, for one reason or another, that keeps nerves alerted, always triggered to fire that *first* fear so intensely.

A Small Voice Says, "Go On!"

Your willingness to try to see panic through means that at least some part of you is going forward. A small voice says, "Go on!" despite a stronger, more persistent voice saying, "No, I can't." You build on that little voice. However faint it may be, it is the seed of acceptance, the beginning of cure.

Even when you succeed in coping with *second* fear, desensitization takes time. With utter acceptance, a sensitized body may still flash *first* fear for some time to come. Some patients have complained that although they no longer panic, they have an inner feeling of apprehension, almost of vibration, as if panic were on the verge of coming. This can be compared to the vibrations of a large bell after it has been struck and as the sound dies away.

Although it is disturbing, one can learn to function with this feeling of inner vibration, near-panic. It gradually passes. A woman wrote, "I soon learned to disregard the trembling feeling that came after the panic ceased. It did not last long." Sensitized nerves heal as naturally as a broken leg, but it takes time. To face and accept one's nervous symptoms without adding *second* fear—how important this is. It works miracles if one is prepared to do just this.

It is not easy to face, accept, and let time pass. It is especially difficult to let time pass because so much time has already been spent in suffering and despair that asking for more time to pass may seem an impossible demand. It is difficult but necessary. Also, don't think I underestimate the severity of your panic. I understand how severe it can be. I also know that even with the help of daily sedation and the best of intentions, you may feel the determination to accept but think yourself too exhausted to do so. It is as if your mind is willing to accept, but your body is too tired to take its orders.

You may, while recovering, have the strange experience of feeling panic and other nervous symptoms and yet at the same time knowing *they no longer matter*. One sufferer wrote, "I still suffered from agoraphobia, but I was not afraid of that anymore. It was just a nuisance." In other words, the feelings lingered because of memory and some remaining sensitization, but she knew how to deal with them.

However long you have been ill, if you make up your mind not to add *second* fear, complete recovery is inevitable. How important it is to unmask panic and see those two separate fears, how important to learn how to recognize *second* fear and send it packing. Recognizing *second* fear and coping with it is the way to desensitization, the way to recovery. I assure you of this.

"Putting Up With"

You must be sure you know the difference between true acceptance and just "putting up with." "Putting up with" means withdrawing from panic in panic, adding panic to panic, hoping that panic will go quickly and not come back—sometimes even hoping it will come so that you can get it over. It means avoiding people and places which bring panic, so that the horizon becomes narrower and narrower until it is eventually bounded by the front gate. It means always leaving a way open for quick retreat; it means expecting retreat; it means continued illness.

True Acceptance

True acceptance means recognizing *second* fear and adding as little of it as possible. Recognizing *second* fear may not be easy at first, but when you are familiar with it, you will be amazed how much *second* fear you have been adding as torture to your daily life. True acceptance means even welcoming panic so you can practice coping with it the way I have advised until it no longer frightens. I can almost hear your groans as you read this, but *you can do it*. I have watched many, many people, just as desperate as you and with no more courage than you think you have, come through panic to peace; so why shouldn't you?

Recently I spoke to a woman whom I first saw three years ago. She had been agoraphobic for twenty years and was so housebound she could not cross her own street alone, could go nowhere without her husband, and even then could drive only a mile or so away from the house. I led her to a nearby park and taught her, after much persuasion, to walk up the pathway by herself. She managed for about fifty yards and returned delighted, although shaking and exhausted.

From time to time, she balked at my teaching. It was too hard (so she thought); it would work for others but not for her! She tried other treatments but finally admitted the only way was to go through panic, as I had taught her. She explained, "One goes through it anyway, so I suppose one might as well do it the right way. At least, that is how I finally saw it!"

If she can do it, you can. No one could have been more frightened and sensitized or have felt more inadequate than that woman when I first saw her. The secret lies in attitude. As soon as she decided she might as well do it the right way, the battle was half won. If you have not succeeded so far, surely this is indication enough that your present attitude must be changed.

"This Doctor Doesn't Know How Sick I Am!"

Do not be tempted to think, "This doctor doesn't know how sick I am!" Can you see how, by thinking this way, you have already added *second* fear, and how insidious that *second* fear can be? When you finally learn to see panic through with true acceptance, you do not need dark glasses, do not have to sit at the back of the auditorium, do not have to walk as far as the corner of the street one week, into the shopping center the next, before you finally graduate to the supermarket. You could go downtown by bus today because by learning how to cope with panic, you take your cure with you wherever you go. So:

- Remember that props have a habit of giving way, so do not placate fear with excuses—face and truly accept it.
- Learn to recognize *second* fear, and practice sending it packing.
- Wait. Do not stoke your fire with *second* fear by tensely withdrawing from panic.
- There is a limit to the intensity of panic even a sensitized body can produce.
- Your mind does not go numb. You can always think, even if only the wrong thoughts.
- You have been bluffed by physical feelings. *First* fear will always die down if you give it time.

- Let *first* fear do its worst, and there will be no mounting panic.
- Build on that little voice.

PALPITATIONS

By palpitations I mean the short abrupt attack of rapidly beating heart which may come occasionally to a nervously ill person. It may occur on exertion or perhaps just as he is dropping off to, or wakening from, sleep. Palpitations when one is in bed and alone at night can be especially alarming. All too often the victim immediately sits up in a panic or lies sweating, hands tingling, face burning, while he waits for some further development, which, he suspects, could even be death. The anxiety of weeks, months, may have so sensitized the nerves of his heart that any noise, any stress—perhaps merely the slamming of a car door in the street or an uneasy dream—anything that wakens him with a start, may be enough to set his heart racing.

If you suffer in this way and are awakened by palpitations, the more you panic, the more adrenaline is released and the longer the attack can last. Although you may think, "I wish the doctor could feel my pulse now; this is terrifying!" were you to take your pulse, you would find your heart is not beating at much more than 120 beats per minute. If any one of us runs for the bus when out of form, our heart may beat just as quickly as during palpitations, and we may be just as conscious of its pounding; but it does not worry us because we understand the cause and know the rapid beating will ease when we stop running.

Most people, however, are frightened by a sudden attack of palpitations, and yet nervous palpitations are not dangerous. The full bursting feeling in the throat is only the unusually strong pulsation of the main arteries in the neck. If you could see how thick and appreciate how powerful your heart muscle is, you would lose all fear of its bursting or being damaged by palpitations. A healthy heart can tolerate a rate of over two hundred beats per minute for days, even weeks, without any damage. So let your heart race until it chooses to calm down, remembering it is a good heart, beating quickly because of nervous stimulation; such stimulation will not harm it, and it will always eventually calm down. I am assuming your doctor has examined your heart and told you your trouble is "only nerves," that "there is nothing wrong with your heart."

Understanding that the palpitations are no more than a temporary upset in the timing of the heartbeat caused by overstimulated nerves and that the attack always calms down will help you lose your fear of them. Less fear means less adrenalin and consequently less excitation, so the attacks come less frequently and, as your health improves, finally cease to come. At all costs resist treating yourself as an invalid.

If you have an attack while out, you may feel more comfortable if you rest until the attack passes. You may continue walking or working, however, if you prefer to do so. While you wait or walk, try to accept the palpitations without recoiling from them, remembering that even while your heart palpitates, nature is working to calm the racing. *So do not turn homeward* in fear. There is no need to hurry home to rest after an attack. I stress once more that this advice is meant only for those whose doctors have examined their hearts and told them their trouble is nervous.

If you are agoraphobic, never let fear of palpitations send you hurrying home; stay in the shop, at the school meeting, in the movie theater. Nature will stop the attack in her own time; *you* do not have to do anything about it except willingly see it through. If you do this, you will be surprised how soon the nervous palpitations will pass.

During recovery, some people learn to accept their palpitations so well that they can turn over and go to sleep during an attack. Others need a pill to help calm them, and I sometimes advise this during the early stages of recovery. I do not ask for stoical forbearance from a severely sensitized person. In the beginning I ask only for an understanding of the harmless nature of nervous palpitations and for as much acceptance, with as little panic, as possible.

CONSTANTLY QUICKLY BEATING HEART

A person under the tension of sustained anxiety may find his heart constantly beating quickly, although not as fast as during an attack of palpitations. As with palpitations, the increased rate is merely nervous reaction, and once again it is the awareness that disturbs, not the actual rate. This constant awareness of the body repeatedly brings the sick person's thoughts back to himself, and he dreads this. His thoughts so often, and too easily, revert to himself. With the most courageous intentions, the woman afraid to leave the house alone may venture out thinking, "I'll really try to make the corner shop today, and I'm not going to think about myself!" So as she walks, she concentrates with great effort on her neighbors' gardens or on passing cars, and once inside the shop, while waiting to be served, glues her eyes to the jars on the shelves and reads each label as it has never been read before. And yet all the time, she feels her heart beating quickly, her body trembling, her legs shaking, until she wonders how much longer she can bear it. The body works on the mind, and the mind then works on the body—the old cycle of despair which may finally drive her out of the shop, unserved.

AFRAID TO NOTICE WHAT IS HAPPENING TO HER BODY

She has been resorting to subterfuge to take her mind off her feelings. That is running away, not facing. No one can work the miracle of calming their body *while they are afraid to notice what is happening to it.* While her body is sensitized, this woman will feel her heart beating quickly, and she will remain sensitized to the beating while she anxiously listens to, and records, each beat or just as anxiously tries not to listen.

NO MAGIC SWITCH TO CALM YOUR HEART IMMEDIATELY

If you suffer in this way, be prepared to live with this quick beating, to accept the racing and thumping as part of the process of recovery, until your nerves become less sensitized. You have made the mistake of thinking that while your heart continues to beat quickly, you must still be ill. It may be weeks before you cease to be conscious of your heart's quick action, but once you accept it, *you will be getting better all the time.* There is no magic switch to calm your heart immediately, although sedatives help.

A constantly quick pulse may have a physical cause—for example, anemia or an overactive thyroid gland. So once again be sure you have your doctor's assurance that your quick rate is nervous.

"Missed" Heartbeats

A heart, stimulated by too much alcohol, nicotine, or caffeine (coffee, tea), irritated by indigestion, or simply nervous tension, may "miss" beats. The beats are not really missed, although it feels as if they are. They are spaced irregularly and are called extrasystoles. Once again, the timing of the beat is at fault. The heart compensates for an unusually quick beat by taking a restful pause, so that the two unevenly spaced beats take the same time as two even beats. The long pause gives the sensation of the heart "stopping" or "missing" a beat. It doesn't.

"Missed" heartbeats are not dangerous. Most people

over forty, and many healthy young people, have them but are unaware of them. In the sensitized person the forceful beat after the long pause may bring an unpleasant feeling —rather like a sudden descent in an elevator—and this can be very disconcerting if there is a long run of extra-systoles, especially if attacks occur frequently. The sufferer may stand still, thinking his heart is about to stop. The heart will not stop because of "missed" beats.

Indigestion—wind around the heart—can aggravate this condition. Exercise abolishes nervous extrasystoles, so do not let them intimidate you into lying on the couch. Some sufferers describe their "missed" beats as fibrillation. Fi-brillation is quite different from extrasystoles. Get your doctor's reassurance about this if you have any doubt.

GIDDINESS

When a housebound person is trying to go out alone, there is nothing more discouraging than a sidewalk that seems to heave, houses that seem to sway, and a body that feels unsteady. The usual response is to sit down and wait for the giddiness to pass or, if no seat is available, to hold onto the nearest support and later to return home and give up trying to leave the house that day. Indeed, giddiness may be such a frequent visitor to the nervously ill woman, even at home, that waiting for a day when she can go out not feeling giddy may mean being house-bound for weeks: hence the plaintive question, "How can I ever leave the house while I am as giddy as this? I have only to think of going out and I am worse."

There are two kinds of giddiness. One, called vertigo, is usually not "nervous" in origin. With true vertigo, sta-tionary objects seem to move rapidly, the room to swirl suddenly. The sufferer may stagger so violently that she may be thrown to the floor. There is usually an organic cause for such violent giddiness—perhaps a small piece of wax stuck to the eardrum, a blocked eustachian tube, and so on. The sufferer eventually consults a doctor.

We are rarely concerned with true vertigo in nervous illness. Here, giddiness is more likely to be the light-headed type. The sufferer feels "floaty," giddy within himself, and is not so conscious of everything spinning violently around. Nervous giddiness is tension giddiness. Tension interferes with the balancing mechanism (semicircular canals of the ears) receiving the correct messages from eye, neck, and body muscles. Although the interference may sometimes be so severe that the victim feels propelled by it, the feeling of propulsion is never as acute as with true vertigo.

The swaying type of giddiness may also accompany low blood pressure or may be felt when high blood pressure temporarily falls—for example, in hot weather, after taking sleeping pills, and so on. It is reassuring to know that giddiness more often follows a fall, rather than a rise, in blood pressure. So many people with high blood pressure, when they have a spell of giddiness, are unnecessarily afraid of a stroke.

"Change of life" may also bring giddy spells, as may bending while gardening, typing, washing hair, or simply rising too quickly from a horizontal position. Most mechanisms misbehave sometimes, so why should we expect a machine as complicated as our body always to function perfectly? As it is, the body gradually adjusts itself to tension giddiness, and it will do so more quickly if we do not add further tension by being afraid of the giddiness. One woman was haunted by the thought of being held up in her car by the red light at intersections. As soon as the green changed to amber she would think, "I daren't stop now! This is where I always have a giddy spell!" So she would rush through the crossing on the amber light, and, of course, this extra tension accentuated any tendency to giddiness. *She had induced her own giddiness.*

Another woman said she was too giddy to walk up the street, but that she could manage very well on her bicycle. She had been able to convince herself she was not giddy while riding because she did not have as much opportunity to concentrate on herself then as she did while walking, and so consequently she was not as giddy. Attitude can work wonders.

INABILITY TO TAKE A DEEP BREATH

So many overanxious people, especially when out, find expanding their chests to take in a deep breath disturbingly difficult. This does not mean their lungs or hearts are diseased but merely that chest muscles are overtensed. They do not understand this feeling and "gasp and gulp" for breath—as one woman described it—half believing that unless they succeed, they will suffocate.

Nature was not so foolish as to make our conscious efforts fully responsible for our breathing; if she had, how would we breathe while asleep or unconscious? We have a respiratory center in our brain which automatically regulates our breathing. If we do not inspire enough oxygen, carbon dioxide accumulates in our blood; when it reaches a certain concentration, this stimulates the breathing center, which then, by means of our involuntary nerves, forcibly expands our lungs to take in more air and wash out the excess carbon dioxide.

To illustrate how automatically this center works I ask a patient disturbed in this way to see how long he can hold his breath—to actually stop breathing. At first he may be reluctant to try such a "dangerous" experiment, but when he does, he is surprised to find that after about half a minute

—the time it takes for carbon dioxide to accumulate— *he is forced to breathe* almost against his will, usually by taking a very deep breath indeed. When he realizes there is a control beyond his control, he often sees the folly of his desperate struggle.

If you suffer from nervous "overbreathing" (hyperventilation), do not let it frighten you. Breathe as shallowly as you feel you must, but do not be concerned with what might happen because you breathe this way. Your respiratory center will see that you inspire deeply enough despite your effort to hinder it. Let this automatic control look after you. It guards you very well at night while you sleep, so why should it fail during the day? It will not fail.

Shallow breathing can temporarily wash out too much carbon dioxide, and so the sufferer may feel giddy and his hands may tingle. This is not a forerunner of a stroke. It means only that the blood has become slightly alkaline because of reduced carbon dioxide, and the body responds to increased alkalinity with giddiness and tingling. The respiratory center soon adjusts this by slowing down breathing until enough carbon dioxide has accumulated to correct the excess alkalinity.

I have sometimes been surprised at how quickly a patient can recover from shallow breathing when he loses his fear of it. A young woman walked into my consulting room, breathing in obvious distress. She was desperate because, as she said, she had been breathing this way on and off for months. My explanation of the respiratory center, and then the experiment of holding her breath, relieved her mind so that she relaxed and began to take deep natural breaths. She has not been troubled by shallow breathing since then.

Do not be disappointed if, despite understanding, you still have occasional difficulty in breathing deeply. It is not important, and acceptance (real acceptance) once more works the miracle by releasing tension.

WEAKNESS ("JELLY LEGS")

The weakness that comes with nervous disturbance is the weakness of emotional shock—the weakness that any of us might feel if told suddenly we had inherited a million dollars. Adrenaline, released by shock, dilates blood vessels in leg muscles, so that blood drains from the rest of our body into these muscles and does not circulate adequately. This brings a feeling of trembling weakness in our legs. The action of adrenaline is well illustrated by its effect on the asthmatic patient. He may have to rest until the weakness (the aftereffect of an injection of adrenaline) has passed.

The agoraphobic woman may have little spasms of panic whenever she thinks of going out alone, so that when she starts off, she is already in "such a state" that any extra strain while out—crossing a main thoroughfare, standing in a line, entering a bus—may immediately bring such a feeling of trembling weakness that her legs seem to turn to jelly, ready to buckle under her. So she thinks, "What is the use of trying today? I might as well go home." It is not difficult to understand why, if she does venture out again, she will begin by timidly testing herself to see if she can get as far as the front gate, then to the end of the street, and so on, without feeling weak. The fear she feels while trying in this way is an open invitation to the feelings she dreads. She has placed herself in the cycle of fear-adrenaline-fear. Just as realization that they have been bluffed by physical feelings has cured some patients, so has understanding the fear-adrenaline-fear cycle.

The nervously ill person sitting in a crowded auditorium continuously gives himself little shocks (extra adrenaline) by thinking, "How much longer can I go through this? What if I faint in front of all these people? I can feel it coming!" —shock after shock. He can usually take onslaught upon onslaught, at worst feeling light-headed. The nervously ill person rarely faints. So relax in this knowledge if you find yourself in a situation where you feel "weak all over."

A PILGRIMAGE FROM CHAIR TO CHAIR

A nervous woman may tire so easily that standing while shopping, especially while waiting to be served, is an ordeal. Shopping becomes a pilgrimage from chair to chair. If no chair is handy, her immediate apprehensions about a weak turn are enough to invite one.

If the shopper were prepared to stand or walk without apprehension, however "charged with lead" her legs might feel, she would find that by the time she had finished, not only would she have recovered but she would also have gained confidence from the effort. As long as she stays apprehensive, fear continues to release adrenaline, and the weakness persists. By disregarding weakness, strength gradually returns.

If you suffer from recurring attacks of nervous weakness, try to remember that the less you worry about your wobbly legs, the less wobbly they will be. "Jelly legs" will still carry you if you will let them, so give them the chance. If your legs feel weak, it is because *they are responding normally to the tension you have been building up.* The weakness and heaviness are only feelings; this is not true organic weakness, so once more do not be bluffed by physical feelings.

SHE SENT HER LEGS THE WRONG MESSAGE

The importance of attitude is well illustrated by one woman who can walk confidently on grass but feels her legs "give way" when she walks on hard pavement. On grass she sends her legs, perhaps subconsciously, the message, "You can walk here," and, of course, they can. On pavement she sends them the signal, "You can't walk here," and her legs react accordingly.

Possibly she had her first attack of weakness while walking on a pavement, and the memory, even subconsciously, may linger to rob her of confidence when walking on a hard surface; or the jarring impact of her heels against the pavement may make her conscious of her legs and so of her fear. This may sound childish, but when a woman (or man) has been through as many weak turns over the years as this woman has, the old tracks of suffering respond uncomfortably readily, and despair follows just as easily. It takes special courage and understanding to come out of such an emotional quagmire. If you suffer this way, *you can do it*. A change in attitude, even though tentative at first, gradually brings a change in strength. Our nervous control of muscles is a double-edged weapon. Muscles strengthen with the right attitude, tremble with the wrong.

WE KEEP OUR GRIP BY LETTING IT GO

It is strange how we keep a grip on ourselves by *being prepared to release it*. We cannot keep the right kind of grip by tensely holding on, as so many wrongly suppose. By abandoning ourselves to whatever our body may care to do, we release the tension that fatigues the nerves controlling muscles and blood vessels, so that they recover their ability to function normally, and strength gradually returns. So much of a nervously ill person's suffering is self-induced through ignorance. It is also induced by the hovering shadow of having someday, somehow, to face what they feel is the *ultimate*. No one is quite sure what he means by this, but each is convinced it is crucial. The *ultimate*—in other words, the worst that could possibly happen—is no more than fear and imagination working together to create a bogeyman, which will disappear if one has the courage to confront it.

Although a sufferer reading this at home may feel hopeful and be prepared to face the worst, it is not so easy to stay reassured during an attack of weakness away from home. The despair of the moment may be so acute that it is difficult to reassure oneself adequately during that moment. If only one's body would respond quickly to one's own reassurance! Instead, it may take quite a while to recover from an attack of weakness. Also, even with understanding and acceptance, because of previous months of tension, weak spells may recur from time to time. This is also part of the strangeness of recovery.

It is only human to remain a little afraid of weak turns and so unwittingly to pave the way for their recurrence. Do not be deterred by nervous weakness. Muscles and mental attitude both strengthen with use.

Some people faint more easily than others, whether nervously ill or not; for example, soldiers are known to faint on parade when they must stand still for long periods, especially in hot weather. This kind of faintness can be corrected by moving one's body as much as the situation permits, so keeping blood circulating. Please do not think, after reading this, that if you have to stand still for any length of time, you must immediately begin to fidget. The nervously ill person who stands quite still for longer than a few minutes would be hard to find.

TOO LITTLE SUGAR IN THE BLOOD

Occasionally a nervously ill, or indeed a non–nervously ill, person uses up the body's available glucose too rapidly, and the level of blood sugar falls below normal. Weakness, with trembling and sweating, may then follow. The nervous person may blame his nerves for this. While these attacks may come from working strenuously, under pressure, especially if one has not had enough to eat during the day, they are not necessarily part of nervous illness and are relieved by eating something sweet. If no food is available, simply resting for ten minutes gives the liver time to release stored glycogen, which is then broken down into glucose. If these turns come frequently, the sufferer should plan his diet to include enough protein—meat, fish, cheese, eggs. The condition is called hypoglycemia.

So:

- Do not be drawn to every chair you see, however charged with "lead" your legs may feel.
- Remember that apprehension releases the adrenaline that helps to bring weakness.
- "Jelly legs" will still carry you if you let them.
- You keep the best grip by being prepared to release it.

FEAR OF VOMITING

I have not known one nervously ill person who has vomited in public. Some are so haunted by this fear, that they refuse invitations to eat with friends or attend any public gathering. Many have gagged gently to themselves or hurriedly left the room to do so outside, but vomit—no. This is surely consoling when we realize that short of putting his finger down his throat, a nervous person could hardly stimulate his vomiting muscles more than he does by his anxious concentration on them. It is not as easy as a nervous person imagines for a healthy stomach, even a nervous stomach, to regurgitate its food. As I mentioned earlier, it is the tense holding on that does the damage, not the letting go. If the nervous person were to give up the struggle to prevent vomiting, his stomach muscles would gradually relax, and not only would he lose his squeamish feeling, but also vomiting would be even less likely. Feel as nauseated and as sick as you must while in the company of others, but be reassured—you will not vomit.

BLUSHING

Intense blushing can be a great trial to many young women and even men; indeed, one middle-aged man came to me for help, saying, "Doctor! I blush at the slightest thing. I don't just go pink. I go a deep scarlet and right down my neck!" He, a European immigrant, would not go to his club because of severe blushing. Each Saturday night he and his wife sat in loneliness—they spoke little English —although she pathetically tried to persuade him to take her to join their friends.

One woman's life became so disrupted by blushing that she would not open the door to strangers. As her husband's business was carried on partly at home, this was not only a handicap to the business but also made her feel so shamefully inadequate that she was beginning to lose confidence in many other ways. Her trouble began during the last war when, as a young girl, she was evacuated to a family in the country. She was a shy child and did blush a little, but at that time she gave this no special attention until one of the older girls in the new family persisted in staring at her during meals, trying to make her blush. She was sometimes too upset to finish her meal and, of course, blushed even more profusely. When she returned to London two years later, intense blushing had become her response to the slightest attention. She carried that cross for twenty years and was the butt of any thoughtless person who crossed her path.

She was cured at last when I explained a blush is caused by the nerves controlling the blood vessels in our face and neck becoming so startled by emotion—fear, anger, shame —that they suddenly release their grip and blood floods into the vessels. Trying not to blush (and this had been her constant aim) means tensely concentrating on one's face when one should be unaware of it. The more attention nerves get, the more easily startled they become, and so, of course, the more likely they are to lose their grip and bring a blush.

When she understood this, I finally persuaded her to let herself blush, whatever the situation—especially at the front door—and to try not to be so upset when she did. It was not easy to persuade her she was capable of coping with this difficulty or that doing it this way would cure her. She thought unless she took a very firm grip, the blushing would surely get worse. When I pointed out that her way of coping in the past had reduced her almost to isolation she agreed to try it my way. I also encouraged her by showing her that it was far more important not to restrict her family's life—as she was now doing—than to care about a stranger's opinion of her, which after all was usually only one of passing amusement. She finally got her priorities right and in three months was opening the front door, sometimes hardly noticing whether she blushed or not. When she saw me at that time, she said she still blushed a little but did not worry about it, because her husband said a little blushing was attractive.

If blushing is your trouble, the less you care whether you blush or not, the less likely you are to blush. The difficulty is not caring. The rest follows if you can manage that.

Some of the people who came to me were bewildered by interpretations made by analysts of their deep blushing, interpretations often with a sexual or guilt basis. The young woman just described had been told hers was due to guilt about a subconscious sexual deviation. She was happily married with children and luckily did not take this interpretation seriously. Her cure by my explanation and her courage alone surely showed how wrong the analyst's suggestion had been. Interpreting deep blushing as an expression of subconscious guilt is a temptation some therapists cannot resist; unfortunately, it has damaging results for people for whom such interpretation is unjustified.

ANY STRANGE NEW FEELING

Beware of adding "Oh, my goodness" to any unexpected disturbing nervous feeling you may experience or of thinking, "This is a new one; the doctor didn't mention this.

This must be important!" It usually is not. Accept any such new feeling that might come; accept anything your body does while you walk, while you work, while you wait. I remind you it is necessary to be examined by your doctor and assured your trouble is nervous.

Understand that you have been frightened for so long that being afraid has become a habit, and therefore during the early stages of recovery you will probably continue to be frightened. No one could banish fear such as yours overnight. Accept even this. Accept that for some time yet you will often add *second* fear, plenty of it. *You will add it from habit.* In the beginning you can only practice not adding it. So when you fail, do not despair too much. Despair, yes—who wouldn't?—but don't utterly despair. The person who eventually recovers completely has learned to disregard failure, to disregard despair.

TAKE THOSE FIRST STEPS SLOWLY

And whether you are agoraphobic or not, take those first steps—whatever they may be—toward recovery at a moderate pace; do not rush. Rushing to "get it over with quickly" only increases agitation, and agitation prepares the way for panic. So go slowly, gently, and do not be afraid to notice how you feel; do not try forcing yourself to think of something different to keep your mind off yourself—you will lose that battle for sure. How could you not notice how you feel, not think of yourself? You have been doing just that for so long; of course you will continue to do it. So accept that you will think continuously about yourself, and be prepared for this also. Be prepared to think and feel anything, go toward it, do not shrink from it, and at the same time try to be not quite so impressed by the way you feel. You have been misled by feelings for such a long time. Actually, your sensitized body is functioning normally in the circumstances you are creating for it.

In circumstances of bewilderment, fear, and tension such as yours, how could your heart not race, your hands not sweat and perhaps tremble; how could you not feel strange, weak, unreal? Therefore be prepared to feel this way in the beginning, and do not expect acceptance to immediately work wonders. As I said, this may be the first time in years that you have tried to go out by yourself or face other difficulties. Isn't it natural you should feel apprehensive, strange, unreal? Aren't these feelings to be expected? Of course they are; they are not even sick reactions. *They are normal reactions under the circumstances.*

SLOW RECOVERY MAY BE GOOD FOR YOU

If you recover quickly by following this advice, that is fine. I have often seen quick recovery. If your recovery is slow, however, do not be disappointed. *Each person must be prepared to recover at his or her own pace.* Slow recovery can be good for you. It gives opportunity to practice again and again the method I teach until you make it part of yourself. Panic rarely vanishes by suddenly ceasing to come. Panic goes only when you take the panic out of panic—that is, *by seeing it through so often without adding second fear that eventually even panic no longer matters.*

If you are agoraphobic, while you are trying to move away from home have the courage to cut the tie between yourself and the house. Release your body by thinking forward. If in a car or a bus, move forward in thought with it. Do not hold yourself back; float forward. Loosen that tense hold.

IN THE FRONT LINE OF BATTLE

Practicing this way could make you feel more tired and "nervier" than ever. This is understandable. While you avoided situations in which you thought you would panic, you could go weeks without panicking, but when you are willing to put yourself into fear-producing situations, you are in the front line of battle, as it were, and may panic more than you have for a long time. It is a rare person who can cope with panic the right way on every occasion in the early stages of recovery. This is why you may be temporarily more sensitized and "nervier" than before and so may need extra tranquilization (prescribed by your doctor) at this time. And this is why some people, when they first practice my teaching, occasionally lose heart and think they are worse, not better.

REFRESH YOURSELF BY MAKING NO EFFORT

Do not be afraid to let a day or two pass without practicing; do not think you will lose all you have gained if you do not practice daily. You will never lose what you have learned once you start to work at recovery the right way. Refreshing yourself sometimes by making no effort for a while is wiser than flogging a tired body for fear you will lose what you learned yesterday. *Accept these halts in recovery.* I speak more about this later.

YOU DID RUSH HEADLONG TO TRY TO "GET IT OVER WITH"

When you fail, try to discover where you went wrong. When you review the situation, I am sure you will find you did rush headlong to try to "get it over with"; you did hurry to get back home; you did withdraw in fear; you did try to sit on panic, to stop its coming; you did add too much *second* fear; or you were so overtired and oversensitized with so much trying, so much endeavor, that you became frightened by the renewed intensity of your fear just when you were expecting to feel better. Maybe you listened to the little voice that is always ready to discourage you, the little voice that says, "You can never do it. The method might be right for others, but you haven't got what it takes to succeed!" How often have I heard of this little voice, and how often have I seen people who were frightened by it at first eventually recover completely. Do not be influenced by that little voice; it speaks in vain to so many.

So when you fail, go out and practice once more, but this time practice the right way. And remember: Practice; do not test yourself. Do not think, for example, "I went round the park so well last week; I wonder how I'll do it today," and then be disappointed if you are more afraid today than you were last week. Your anxiety to do as well as you did last week could make you begin the journey round the park just a little more fearfully than you did a week ago, so that it takes only a minor incident to throw you into panic and to bring disappointment instantly. The way to recovery is rather tricky, isn't it? This is especially true if you take every baffling twist and turn seriously. Accept it all. Do not waste energy trying to work out why you managed so well one day and so badly the next. Accept it until the meaning of true acceptance is written on your heart.

Following this advice is not easy, but I assure you you can do it. If you continue to accept despite setback, despite disappointment, despite despair, you will find that the weakness, the panic—all the feelings you dislike so much—will gradually come to mean less and less. As they mean less, they grow less intense and come less often because they depend on your dislike of them to incite your nerves to bring them. They depend on your dislike of them for their very existence. Utter acceptance removes anxiety, removes bewilderment, removes tension, and so removes the symptoms of stress and *your symptoms are no more than the usual symptoms of stress,* however unique they may seem to you.

So:

- Take those first steps at a moderate pace. Do not rush.

- Accept that you may frighten yourself for some time to come—until habit dies and sensitization improves.
- Be prepared to think and feel anything. Let come what will.
- Do not be bluffed by any new strange nervous feeling.
- Accept halts in recovery.
- Do not waste energy trying to work out why you managed so well one day and so badly the next.
- Let true acceptance be written on your heart.

The journals give in more detail treatment of many aspects of the anxiety state, including agoraphobia in particular.

4

Unraveling the Maze of Nervous Experiences

Indecision, suggestibility, loss of confidence, feelings of unreality and of personality disintegration, that dreaded morning feeling, sleeplessness, obsession, and depression are described in detail, along with their treatment, in my earlier book, *Hope and Help for Your Nerves*. These experiences are so important in nervous illness and cause such suffering, confusion, and bewilderment that it is necessary to discuss them at least briefly here and point out how logically they arise and how simply they can be explained.

INDECISION

Because constant fear and tension have sensitized nerves to produce exaggerated emotions, the slightest change of mind when trying to make a decision can be accompanied by such strong emotional reaction that decision seems impossible. Each point of view appears equally important, equally right one minute and yet equally wrong the next. Even the simplest decision may seem too much.

A patient once said, "I used to tie myself in knots thinking: Should I do this or shouldn't I? Whatever I did, I worried and thought I shouldn't have done it. Now I act, and that's that. Mind you, when I'm in a setback, I go back to the old state of shilly-shally, and I can't let the 'whys' drop away easily either!" He continued, "Sometimes I say to my wife, 'Say something quickly, Mary.' This is when I'm in such a state I can't make my mind up about anything. Any suggestion Mary makes I cling to."

Making a decision is especially difficult when the ill person is depleted and at the same time is trying to decide how far he can trust his strength. He doesn't want to overdo things, and yet the strain of inactivity is almost impossible to bear. When I discussed this with the same patient, he said, "That is exactly how I felt a while back. My wife and I went for a run down the coast when I was on vacation, and after we arrived, I spent hours trying to decide whether to stay the night or come home. One minute I thought I was too tired to make the journey back, and yet I couldn't bear the thought of staying. As soon as I turned the car round toward home, I felt so exhausted at the thought of the trip I was sure we should have stayed. But if we had decided to stay, I know I would have immediately thought we should have gone." Thought and feeling so closely tied! Each point of view right one moment and yet equally wrong the next!

SUGGESTIBILITY

A sensitized person can be easily misled into thinking any suggestion that brings such strong reactions as he feels must be important. He becomes suggestible to so much. Reading a newspaper can be a real hazard. A report on illness, especially nervous illness, so impresses him that it can upset him for days. He thinks that if he hasn't already had all the described symptoms, he soon will have.

A young girl asked me, "Why do the wrong ideas always come with such force and the right ones seem so shaky?" The wrong suggestions produce fear, and fear is felt so acutely that it can override other feelings. It is because the negative, destructive suggestions carry such threat and therefore come with such force that they cling tenaciously and are so often mistaken for truth.

The right ideas seem shaky because in a nervous person they have such an insecure foundation; they come only in glimpses. Hope, the feeling the sufferer needs so badly, is a good example of this, for it is so tentative.

LOSS OF CONFIDENCE

Indecision and suggestibility, together with the confusion they bring, must surely lead to loss of confidence. How could they not? Can you see how the pattern unfolds? It becomes a logical pattern when we understand how exaggerated emotions can delude us.

The nervous person is not necessarily always without confidence. He can swing from lacking it to being almost elatedly confident. This in itself is confusing. It seems there is no middle of the road for him.

One man, describing his vacation, said, "It was the last day before coming home. There I was, contemplating: Would I go fishing, or wouldn't I? I looked at the sea and thought, No, it's too rough! It wasn't really rough. I was trying to trick myself. All of a sudden I thought, I'm going!

"So out I went on my own, and I had the most exhilarating time when I got out there. I caught a lot of fish, and coming in, I deliberately let the boat roll about in the sea; and I can remember wading, pushing the boat in front of me with fantastic energy, and yet two hours earlier I had been shaking like jelly at the thought of going." He paused and said quietly, "To get over this you really have to distrust your own mind, don't you?"

I explained, "You distrust what it has been saying to you during the years you have been ill. You have good cause. They are the messages that have been keeping you ill. This is why I teach floating past obstructive thought."

He answered, "It's like giving yourself the wrong signals. Now you want me to try to give myself the right ones."

This man was second in charge of an important national industry. So many of my patients, like him, were confident and successful before they became ill, and many held responsible positions as teachers, managers, executives. They usually struggled to keep working despite their illness, and to do so while they felt so inadequate and were trying to hide their feelings took a lot of courage.

To regain confidence many needed only insight into the reason for their loss of it and an understanding of sensitization, with a program for desensitization. The return of confidence was automatic as time and acceptance reduced their symptoms of stress to normal intensity. They were usually relieved to learn regaining confidence need not be a special objective—that it would return naturally after desensitization.

If nervous illness has been caused by worry that includes personal failure of some kind—perhaps dismissal from work—the confidence lost in this way certainly has to be rebuilt. And, of course, the nervous person who has never been self-reliant finds recovery more difficult because while he learns how to desensitize himself, he must at the same time build up a confidence he has never had. I discuss this in more detail in Journal 3.

AGITATION—WAITING MAY SEEM UNBEARABLE

Continuous strain can also bring agitation. After waiting an hour in the outpatients' department of a busy psychiatric clinic, many an agitated patient leaves before being seen by the doctor. Of all nervous symptoms, agitation is perhaps the most difficult to bear. It needs immediate relief, and this means medication.

UNREALITY

The nervously disturbed person naturally pays more and more attention to what is happening within himself and less and less to outside events. When desperately concerned with our own affairs, it is not easy for any one of us to be interested in a neighbor's new stereo. It is even more difficult for a nervously ill person, whose anxious thoughts are almost compulsively bound within himself. It is this narrowing of interest that leads to his feeling of withdrawal from the outside world—as if there is a veil between it and him, a veil he can neither lift aside nor break through.

"AM I LOSING MY MIND, DOCTOR?"

It is not unusual to hear a patient say, "I cannot make contact with other people. I feel they're in one world and I'm in another unreal world. It doesn't matter how hard I try; I can't find my way back into their world, the world I used to belong to. Am I losing my mind, Doctor?" He may have this feeling of unreality in flashes, or it may seem to be always with him.

A nervously ill person can feel unreal in different ways. He may say, "I feel outside myself, watching myself," or, "When I touch things, I *know* I'm doing it but can't *feel* I'm doing it." Another will say, "It doesn't seem right, or real, to hear somebody laughing." Happiness has become remote to him because his world of introspection has been full of suffering for so long. Others will say, "I listen to people talking, but half the time I see their mouth move and don't hear what they say. It's like looking at TV with the sound turned off."

MEMORY ALONE WILL BRING IT BACK

When the cause of feelings of unreality is explained as no more than the natural result of so much anxious introspection, a nervously disturbed person can be so relieved to know he is not going out of his mind that he loses his fear of it. This sudden release can make him feel more real, more part of the outside world, than he has felt for a long time. This newly gained feeling of reality can be short-lived, however. The previous experience of feeling unreal is so close that it is only natural in his sensitized state that it will return. Memory alone will bring it. And when it comes again, many make the mistake of being upset and thinking that the cause, for them, must be very deep-seated indeed. A nervously ill person is easily influenced by his feelings of the moment; they are hard to bear and therefore make such an impression that they assume an unnecessary importance.

So if a feeling of unreality is part of your suffering, be prepared to work and live with it, and accept that for the time being it is natural to feel this way. Feeling unreal is not in the least important and does not mean that you are "going mental." With understanding, tension eases, and you will gradually find you are becoming less interested in what is happening to you and more interested in the outside world. You become more outward than inward bound.

OBSESSION—KEEPING UNWANTED THOUGHTS AT BAY

Even obsession fits logically into the pattern and so loses some of its nightmarish quality. Obsession may come when mental fatigue is added to sensitization. Unfortunately, few people understand how brain fatigue works. Frightening thoughts cling, and the bewildered sufferer usually makes the mistake of trying to push them away or to replace them with other thoughts. Occasionally he may be successful, but more often the more he tries to forget, the more stubbornly the unwelcome ideas cling. As I have said before, discarding a thought at will can be difficult, especially when the thought is upsetting and the mind tired. And yet this is what the nervous person so often demands of himself. No wonder he despairs when he tries desperately to keep unwanted thoughts at bay.

So many obsessions in nervous illness begin this way. They are no more than unwanted habits established by fear and mental tiredness, and in my experience with my patients, they *seldom have a deep-seated significance*. The nervously ill mother is naturally enough afraid of accidentally harming her child while she is disturbed and lacks confidence and concentration. And she is so suggestible that the thought that she *might* can so easily become the fear that she *will*. This does not mean she is an aggressive type, as some of my patients had been previously told. She is usually no more than a loving but frightened mother with an illness that is following a usual course. This particular fear is shared by so many disturbed mothers; surely they could not all be aggressive.

Unfortunately, such a woman may be—to her chagrin—convinced she must be peculiar because in addition to her fear of harming her child, she can no longer *feel* love for it or, indeed, for any of the family. Actually, she is too emotionally drained to register such an uplifting, expansive emotion as love. Everyday emotions depend on vitality for expression, and fear may have robbed her of vitality. It is paradoxical that whereas she can feel frightening and unhappy emotions intensely, other emotions seem frozen. She invariably takes this temporary depletion seriously, and this adds to her feeling of unreality. Similarly, a nervously ill person may complain of being unable to contact his religion or find comfort in prayer. This can cause havoc to a person dedicated to a religious life.

THOUGHTS CAN BE GROTESQUE

Thoughts can be grotesque when one is anxious. And the stranger, more unreal, even more frightening they seem, the more one may feel compelled to follow them through, almost as if mesmerized, determined to find out the worst.

Whatever your thoughts, however strange, try not to be upset by them. Accept them as normal in your present state, not as something to be dreaded and avoided. Do not make the mistake of supposing there are certain thoughts you must not think, as if there is part of your brain you must not use. Use it all, even the part holding an obsession, and shrink from none of it.

Do not be frightened by your thoughts, however severe the compulsion that may accompany them. Severe tension can give such driving force to some thoughts that they seem to lock their victim in submission. Even here, *never forget they are only thoughts,* no matter how real and compelling they seem at the moment.

It is the fear, not the thoughts, that tenses, sensitizes, tires. It does not matter how much you dwell on yourself or what you think if you try not to do it fearfully. I am not suggesting one can wipe from one's mind nagging thoughts related to a special problem. When a problem is urgent, the advice to "Stop worrying and forget about it" is fatuous. The problem must be faced (see Chapter 5).

FEELING OF PERSONALITY DISINTEGRATION

Surely it is not surprising to hear a nervously ill person say he feels as if his personality were disintegrating or has disintegrated, when he

- finds it difficult to make a decision,
- finds it easy to fall victim to suggestion,
- finds it difficult to have confidence in himself,
- is bewildered by unreality and perhaps by obsession,
- and, in addition, is buffeted by the physical symptoms of stress.

To quote my earlier book, "He has no inner strength on which to depend, no inner self from which to seek direction . . . no inner harmony holding thought, feeling, and action together." Just as confidence returns with desensitization and understanding, so reintegration follows the return of confidence. One does not need to strive for reintegration; one needs to understand and accept apparent disintegration without becoming afraid of, or bewildered by, it.

None of the experiences discussed (with the exception of obsession) needs separate treatment. To select each and treat it individually is to confuse and complicate. Understanding through explanation—such as given here—can by itself restore inner harmony.

Indecision, suggestibility, loss of confidence, feelings of unreality, agitation, personality disintegration, and obsession are tiring emotions; and the sufferer, harassed by them for months, may gradually deplete his reserves of energy and feel apathetic and depressed. Apathy can be so severe he may have no wish even to bathe himself, much less recover. As part of Journal 6, I discuss nervous depression in detail.

So there is the pattern, beginning with indecision and ending with depression; each stage logically follows the other, and each originates from exaggerated emotional reaction to bewilderment and fear. To those who do not understand, it is often a bewildering maze of one tortured moment after another. And yet as each stage followed the other to increase suffering, so with enlightenment and acceptance can one stage after the other dissipate into final peace.

THE EVERLASTING WHY? WHY? WHY?

You may think I stress acceptance too much. You may be skeptical about the simplicity of this approach or may have hoped for a more impressive treatment, especially one that does not leave so much for you to do. I stress acceptance because I have seen it cure where all else failed. I have seen it cure people after more than forty years of their trying one different method after another. Indeed, *I have not seen it fail.* Of course, acceptance is made easier by understanding, and this I am trying to give you.

RISING ABOVE A SITUATION

Consider how acceptance works. It brings a less tense approach; emotions have a chance to calm a little, and there is release from asking the everlasting Why? Why? Why? So mental fatigue gradually lifts. The mind becomes more "flexible," and when one is no longer confined to one point of view, a situation is more easily kept in perspective. This is the meaning of "rising above a situation." It is as if the sufferer becomes two people—the first suffering and the second looking on, reconciled to the suffering and also reconciled to trying to accept it. In other words, the second person rises above the suffering. So think what you will, but remember to do this with as much acceptance as you can manage, not only up to but also *right through* the climax of intensity.

5

Solving the Apparently Insoluble Problem

So far I have talked about people made, and kept, ill by fear of their nervous symptoms and experiences rather than by any special problem. Many people are ill because of some overwhelming problem, however. I discuss here how an apparently insoluble problem (and this includes sorrow, guilt, and disgrace) can cause nervous illness and how one can recover if already made ill in this way.

HOW THE PROBLEM CAUSES ILLNESS

The person who puts himself in danger of nervous breakdown neither solves his problem nor compromises. He spends most of his time dwelling unhappily on the unbearable aspects of his difficulty, torn by indecision and despair. The more anxiously he broods, the tenser he becomes, and because so much constant tension sensitizes his nerves to exaggerate his feelings, his anxiety grows more acute as time passes. His sensitized nerves may in addition bring the well-known pattern of stress symptoms (churning stomach and so on). These are so accentuated when he thinks of his problem that concentration on it becomes more and more difficult, decision more elusive, until tension mounts to bring such agitation that the simplest strain can seem too much to bear.

Sensitization can exaggerate other emotions as well as anxiety. An event formerly thought sad may now seem tragic. A nervously ill medical student, on duty in an outpatients' department, hearing an old woman coughing because of no more than chronic bronchitis, was so moved that he wondered how he would find the fortitude to continue practicing medicine. Such experiences are exhausting and may leave little energy for interest in work or even for interest in living. The sufferer is bewildered by this change within himself and tries hard to get back to being the person he used to be.

To summarize: By constant anxious brooding on an apparently insoluble problem, the sufferer has sensitized his nerves to register upsetting bodily symptoms that frighten him, exaggerated emotions that perplex him, agitation that disturbs him. All this may finally so exhaust him that he becomes apathetic, depressed.

In addition, constant anxious brooding may gradually slow down thinking until thoughts come haltingly. Also, a tired mind has a tendency to revert continuously to one theme. Whereas in the beginning the sufferer could dismiss at will thoughts about his problem, now, because of a fatigued mind, it may seem impossible to forget it even for a moment.

This effort in thinking freely makes it increasingly difficult for him to consider his problem flexibly, from different points of view. By now he is able to see it only from the one disturbing aspect he has been holding constantly before his eyes during the last months. Indeed, when he thinks of his problem, this upsetting point of view may strike so forcibly that he feels completely submerged by it.

Feeling no longer in control of his thoughts or emotions, he sometimes thinks he is going mad. He will clutch desperately at every moment when he feels normal; for example, at times when watching television with the family, he may suddenly feel at peace and think, "This is me at last! If I can stay like this, I'll be all right!" He clings to such moments, afraid to let them go, for fear that if he loses them, he will lose himself.

For a while after such an experience he may feel safe and calm. Because his anxiety has been so intense during the past months, however, he has only to be anxious once more—which is inevitable under the circumstances—and his reactions will be just as alarming as ever. They must be. His sensitized nerves are triggered to make them so. Naturally, when he panics again, he tries yet harder to grasp outside familiar things to steady himself, to contact reality, to reassure himself all is well. His spirits rise one minute but fall the next. He is now afraid and bewildered *by the state he is in* and still has to cope with the original problem. Indeed, he may now be as much concerned with the way he feels as with the problem itself. Surely this description shows how constant anxious brooding, when accompanied by fear and lack of understanding, can bring nervous illness—because by now this person is undoubtedly nervously ill.

RECOVERY

To recover, the person made ill by some apparently insoluble problem must first understand that sensitized nerves can exaggerate both emotions and the physical symptoms of stress: tears come too readily, laughter may be hysterical, the heart races, the stomach churns. He must then understand the tricks brain fatigue can play by slowing down thinking and grooving thoughts in a compulsive way. Above all, he must then follow understanding with acceptance. He can help calm himself temporarily by using tranquilizers prescribed by his doctor, but he must give himself the best tranquilizers of all—understanding and acceptance.

He must be prepared to think as slowly as his tired mind allows and not panic because he cannot think clearly or because he forgets easily. He must not grasp tensely, fearfully, at those moments when he feels normal, afraid to release them for fear of never contacting them again. He must be prepared to let them come and let them go as they will. Acceptance releases some tension, enough to begin desensitization. When this happens, he is no longer so much at the mercy of his physical reactions and can look at his problem more calmly, more rationally, and so by degrees give it all his attention.

HE MUST FIND A NEW POINT OF VIEW

Since he has made himself ill by so much brooding on his problem, we may assume no satisfactory action could have been taken; otherwise he would surely have taken it. If no action be possible, he must find a less painful way of looking at the situation. *He must find a new point of view.*

A nervously ill person can rarely do this unaided because, as already mentioned, his way of thinking has become conditioned by his tense concentration. Every time he thinks of his problem, the established upsetting way of looking at it projects itself immediately and interferes with balanced, calm reasoning. As I said in my earlier book, *Hope and Help for Your Nerves,* he needs a wise counselor, whether it be doctor, religious adviser, or friend, to review the problem dispassionately and help him find a viewpoint that will at least bring some peace.

A different way of looking at the problem acts like a crutch for his tired mind. This new approach may not be entirely to his liking, but it must to some extent satisfy him. Peace of mind cannot be forced, so it is essential that the new point of view bring a minimum of pain and fear. A wise counselor will see to this. A wise counselor will also need patience because the nervously ill person may be so mentally tired that he finds it difficult to hold the new viewpoint for long. He may see it clearly while discussing it but may quickly lose his grasp on it when alone and have to discuss the new approach with his adviser many times before he can accept it as his own.

If he can glimpse the new point of view for a few moments each day, he will have made a beginning. Indeed, this is the beginning. He may repeatedly lose that glimpse and often despair; but if he perseveres, the glimpse will gradually grow clearer and steadier and last longer, until it becomes the established compromise to bring peace at last.

HOW GLIMPSING WORKS

A man or woman with high blood pressure may be obsessed with worry about it and continually dwell on the thought of a stroke. Sometimes such a person will say, "I almost wish the wretched thing would come and get it over with!" A person with such worry needs repeated assurance, and here I have found tape recordings of consultations very helpful.

First, every practical explanation to allay fear should be given; for example, it should be explained to the sufferer that most of the symptoms a layman thinks are due to high blood pressure usually are not. It is possible to have a pressure so high that, in medical language, it is "off the machine" and yet feel no symptoms. The headaches commonly thought due to high blood pressure are more often caused by nervous tension than by the pressure itself. Giddiness can be caused by a sudden fall in blood pressure and is not a sign of an impending stroke.

Having reassured the sufferer about his symptoms, I point out that, though some insurance companies put a high premium on high blood pressure, most people live for years with it. One patient whose pressure was high at seventy died at ninety-seven of pneumonia. So a sufferer should understand that he might live many years with his pressure, especially if helped by the advanced treatment of today, and then might eventually die from some other complaint.

Living with a fear of high blood pressure may take a lot of adjustment—glimpsing—these days, when a layman is subjected to such a barrage of well-intentioned but sometimes misinformed pseudomedical articles in magazines and newspapers. On some days a patient will come into my office happy because he has the right point of view well in focus. On other days, after reading one of these articles, his focus will have slipped, and he will be depressed again. If he persists in practicing glimpsing the right attitude, however, he eventually becomes philosophical enough to take his "pressure tablets" without worrying any more than any of us would, and naturally his physical condition benefits.

At first, glimpsing another approach to some difficult problem may seem impossible because the nervous person feels pulled so strongly toward the old point of view. Also, many different aspects of a problem may disturb a person; indeed, there could be several different problems. Once the sufferer has become sensitized, dormant problems can raise their heads; he may successfully glimpse one aspect, one problem, only to find himself immediately grappling with another. They occur almost in rotation, like a wheel continually turning. If he persists, however, even this tempestuous experience will pass, and he will find he has finally steered himself into calmer waters.

To cope with an apparently insoluble problem:

- understand and try not to be so upset by physical nervous symptoms or by exaggerated emotional reactions;
- try not to be upset if constant brooding slows down thinking, grooves thought, affects memory; and
- practice glimpsing the problem from a different point of view.

6

Do—Don't Just Think
about Doing

You may often need encouragement and, most important of all, may need to be shown where you continue to make the mistakes holding up progress. These mistakes often are:

1. You accept 99 percent of your symptoms and experiences but withdraw from the final 1 percent.
2. You let a setback throw you into complete despair.
3. You are so paralyzed by thinking about doing that you put off the actual doing.

YOU ACCEPT 99 PERCENT BUT WITHDRAW FROM THE FINAL 1 PERCENT

I have explained before how acceptance acts by gradually reducing the tension that keeps nerves sensitized and how sensitized nerves magnify ordinary emotions and stress symptoms. I have explained how, even with complete acceptance, it takes time for sensitized nerves to heal and finally record emotions at normal intensity. You may have understood it all and set out to practice what I taught you but may have found the actual doing so much harder than

it seemed when reading about it or listening to my records *
*because during the critical moment of greatest suffering
you withdrew, you recoiled.*

When you tensely withdrew, your body released more
stress hormones, which increased sensitization, so you
instinctively sought relief by running away from the situation. The next time you set off to practice acceptance, and
I am not talking only about agoraphobia, *watch for the
moment of recoil and go toward it* in a loose, floating
kind of way. That is the key.

An airplane pilot recently explained that the same principle held in his work. When a plane is going into a fall
—a ground loop—one of the hardest lessons for a beginner
to learn is to head the plane into the direction of the fall
and not try to recover balance by tipping the wings in
the opposite direction. To draw away like that is fatal;
to go with the fall is to flatten out and recover balance.
To choose a more common experience, those of us who
ride a bicycle know that when we are about to fall, if we
turn the wheel in the direction of the fall, the bicycle
rights itself; if we turn it in the opposite direction—as
beginners invariably do—we fall.

You may fail in the beginning, perhaps often, but you
will eventually succeed if you recognize the old enemy
withdrawal and do not let it take charge of the situation,
as you have been doing. Watch that last 1 percent. Passing
through that last 1 percent can turn part acceptance into
full acceptance and cure. Never forget: *You make your
own crisis by withdrawal.*

Peace lies on the other side of panic.
Withdrawal is your jailer.
Pass through that last 1 percent.

* An album of two long-playing records, *Hope and Help for Your
Nerves,* written and narrated by Dr. Weekes, is available from Galahad
Productions, P.O. Box 5893, Lake Charles, Louisiana 70601, for $12.00

You Let a Setback Throw You into Complete Despair

Being bogged down by setback is another form of withdrawal. Memory is always ready to defeat you by reminding you of so many other defeats. However far you may sink into setback, never lose the desire to go forward again to recovery. Do not be put off by the places and experiences you fear. These are your salvation *because recovery lies in such places and such experiences.*

WHAT IS RECOVERY?

Recovery is the final establishment of the right attitude of mind. You can practice thinking the right way, however deep you may find yourself in setback. It is difficult to switch from despair to quiet, determined hope, *but you can do it.*

Thousands have despaired as you have and yet have changed their attitude to finally recover. You have as much courage as they. Courage is not given to one and denied another. The difference is some draw on the courage given them; others do not. Courage has never failed to come to those who really want it. The secret lies in that *"really."* So do not let any setback bluff you into refusing to practice again.

Also, do not be disappointed if the symptoms and fears which come with setback stay acute for a while, even when you truly accept them. When you resensitize yourself by being afraid of setback, more time must be allowed for this added sensitization to heal and for your slight grip on hope to strengthen again. In the beginning it is as if each setback must run a certain prescribed course before it spends itself. Accept this also.

Recovery lies in the places you fear.
Seek them with utter acceptance.

YOU ARE PARALYZED BY CONTEMPLATION

You may shrink from the thought of recovery in the future and the demands it may bring. You imagine meeting those demands as you feel now—ill. Let me remind you again that recovery brings its own change. It brings renewed strength, renewed interest, and with these comes ability to cope. Go forward with trust in this change; trust in a gradual merging into normal living. It is the gradualness that makes all possible, but it is this very gradualness that is so hard to bear because it is so frustrating. Also, gradualness allows so much time for contemplation, and during the early stages of recovery *contemplation is the killer.* Over such a long time imagination has flashed so many difficulties in the way of recovery that these have come to seem so concrete they cannot be talked or thought away by you. Only repeated doing will iron them out; *only repeated doing will take the fear out of contemplation.*

My words can only show the way. Also, your understanding is still possible only in thought. Feeling it in your heart as certainty is another matter, and experience alone can put certainty in your heart. Your experience has been so slight so far that you have probably only occasionally glimpsed success. This is hard to bear because it makes you impatient to grasp and hold what you have glimpsed, and patience is never a nervous person's strong point.

So do not be disheartened if at this stage you simply cannot see yourself doing this or that. The thought of it may seem a hopeless dream. And yet salvation lies in repeated doing. It lies in doing until the habit of doing is so well established that it replaces the habit of defeatist thinking. This takes time and effort. The habit of defeatist thinking is so strong that although you may have made many successful journeys or accomplished many difficult tasks by now, deciding to try again may sometimes seem as difficult as ever. Try not to be disturbed by this. Let more time pass until more and more achievement accumulates to bring finally the certainty you crave.

YOU CAN'T POSTPONE THE SCHOOL MEETING

Do not wait for the best moment to make that special effort. The school meeting on the fifteenth may come at a particularly bad moment for you, but you cannot postpone the meeting. The more often you practice my teaching when you do not feel your best, the more confident you will gradually become in facing anything at any time, *however you may feel*. This is the only way for making an appointment or embarking on any undertaking in the future seem less menacing. *Wait on no mood*. It's the sitting and waiting, with hat and coat on and handbag clutched tight, while contemplating moving that is so devastating. Don't let contemplation shackle you. You can still succeed, however "bad" you feel before the actual time of "doing." The confidence you gain by succeeding when you feel your worst is the most invaluable, enduring, dependable confidence of all.

Recovery brings its own strength.
Only repeated doing takes fear out of contemplation.
Salvation lies in repeated doing.
Wait on no mood.

7

Eight Quarterly Journals

These journals are based on those written during 1968–1970 as additional help for certain sufferers from nervous illness who were using my book *Hope and Help for Your Nerves* and my long-playing records. As the journals were written at quarterly intervals, the reader had three months between issues to assimilate and practice the teaching. It may help the present reader to know this so that he does not expect too much from himself in one reading.

JOURNAL 1: Why Recovery Seems So Difficult for So Many Nervously Ill People

WHY RECOVERY SEEMS SO DIFFICULT FOR SO MANY NERVOUSLY ILL PEOPLE

By "nervously ill," I mean people who suffer from excessive anxiety, panic, fears, and upsetting physical nervous symptoms—in other words, people who have been *examined by their doctor* and told they are suffering from "nerves." Before beginning, I would like you to understand I realize I am talking to a mixed group of people—young, middle-aged, old; men and women; those ill for a long time, those ill for a short time; some with special problems; some agoraphobic, others not agoraphobic. I assure you I will bear this in mind and will endeavor to include something in each talk for each of you.

I am aware of your different kinds of fears. Knowing how susceptible you are to suggestion, I will be very careful how I speak about those fears. There will be nothing frightening in these journals, I assure you.

AGORAPHOBIA

First, the word "agoraphobia": It simply means fear of traveling far from home, fear of being where help cannot be had quickly, loss of confidence in being able to manage one's reactions in crowded places, and so on. Agoraphobia is only one of the many aspects of nervous illness. Isn't it natural that people who have weak "turns" when out should eventually avoid going out? Of course it is. And once they do this, they could be called agoraphobic.

Personally, I do not like labels and rarely mention the word "agoraphobia" to my patients. By defining it in this way, it assumes unwarranted specialization and so seems to take on unnecessary importance. It is no more than one phase of a general anxiety state. Whether it is labeled or not, I wish to assure you it is curable. Do not be depressed by anything you may read or hear to the contrary. So much depends on the person treating it as well as on the person seeking cure. I have seen many patients cured after more years of suffering than some of you may have lived. So cheer up!

PROBLEMS

Those of you with special problems may think, "All this is very well, but Dr. Weekes can't help me with my particular problems." I may not be able to help with your individual problems—limited as I am to contacting you through journals alone—but I can show you certain general aspects of recovery which will help you. For example, in addition to being upset by your special problems, worrying about them too much, and for too long, brings its own emotional and physical suffering, which is common to all who suffer as you do. By helping you understand and cope with this, you will at least be relieved of part of your burden and so be able to approach your problems more whole-mindedly and perhaps not be so overcome by them.

THE NIGHT AT THE NEIGHBORHOOD BAR

A nervously ill person is not easy to live with, and in time a once-sympathetic family may begin to react unsympathetically. The husband may become almost as "nervy" as the sick wife, and so he may take to staying late at night at the neighborhood bar. He may also start harassing his wife to "snap out of it," trying to push her, hurry her forward, to recovery. Tension builds up between them. Her inability to move without him, even her reluctance to move with him, gradually changes her relationship with him from companionship to dependency; this is a torture to her and an exasperation to the husband. Relationships with in-laws, even relationships with one's own parents, brothers, sisters, may become strained.

With recovery, these difficulties ease, so try not to be too depressed by them now. It is ironic that some of the problems helping to keep you ill would not be there if you were not ill. They are encouraged by the state you are now in, although you may not recognize this. They automatically resolve themselves as you recover.

DO YOU KNOW WHAT RECOVERY REALLY MEANS?

When most nervous people think of recovery, *they imagine a completely peaceful body* and think that while their body continues to have any nervous symptoms, they must still be ill, that their reactions are sick reactions and would not be there if they were well. Let us be quite clear about this. The monsters that plague the nervously ill person's life are the usual reactions to stress any of us may feel from time to time. They plague the nervous person because they are exaggerated by his sensitization—not simply because they are present. *It is the exaggeration that is the sickness, not the presence.* Let me illustrate this.

Suppose you hear a high-pitched sound. It is not nice but not so very disagreeable, so you go on working. Intensify this sound until it becomes extremely loud, and it may then seem so unbearable that it prevents your working. *Yet it is the same sound, only louder.* So it is with the physical sensations of nervous illness. They are the same normal reactions we all feel to any stress that may come during our day, but to the nervously ill person they are so much, shall we say, louder that they may seem almost unbearable.

Recovery lies not in completely ridding oneself of these reactions—as so many believe—*but in reducing them to normal intensity and normal frequency.* By "normal frequency" I mean being able to quiet your body enough so that nervous responses do not come at every provocation, as they do now—at a thought, an anxious memory; in other words, so that you have some insulation between you and stress.

NORMAL REACTION IS TRICKING HIM

The nervously ill person is blinded to the road to recovery because he does not recognize the *basis of normality* in his strange feelings. This is one of the main reasons why he feels lost. He goes round in circles, trying to rid himself of something that is normal under the circumstances, something that, in a milder form, must always be part of his daily life while he is alive. He would have to be anesthetized, unconscious, sound asleep, to feel no stress and so to be rid of all nervous symptoms!

Even those not nervously ill must have some variation in their normal daily nervous reactions. For example, on some days reaction to any stress will seem more severe than on others. Of course, this natural variation also comes to the nervously sick person, but does he accept it as normal and to be expected? Not he! On the days when his reactions are more severe, he thinks he must be more ill and thrashes himself with added despair and depression. Normal variation in daily nervous reaction is another puzzling pitfall on the way to recovery, and it is a pitfall that never fails to trap a sick person into trying to find a reason for it.

IT MAY BE SO LONG SINCE HE WAS WELL

All this is so understandable because it may be so long since the nervously ill person was well that he may have forgotten what it felt like to be well. He forgets the natural nervous reactions he had then because they did not bother him. He accepted them as part of his day, even expected them. At some time or other most variations had occurred, even the palpitations on running upstairs, the churning stomach before asking the boss for a raise or before taking an examination.

Because he fails to see this basis of normality in the nervous reactions he has now, he is misled into struggling to throw them off completely or into trying to stop them from coming. No one can completely throw off normal reactions, especially when they are exaggerated. So he is tricked into trying to do the impossible. Is it any wonder recovery seems so difficult to so many nervously ill people?

AT THE HEAD OF HIS CLASS

Here is a practical example. Suppose after much sacrifice on her part, a mother hears her son's grades are all A's and that he is at the head of his class. When she first hears the news, might her heart not pound a little and beat faster, her hands tremble? Might she not break out into a sweat, her face flush? Might she not leave her lunch untouched because her excitement has taken away her appetite, be breathless, go "weak all over" and have to sit down for a while? Surely each of these feelings taken separately could be described as unpleasant, and yet she feels them as part of happiness. Her interest is so firmly fixed on her son's success that she hardly notices what is happening to her physically. Her inner feeling of joy is so acute that the stressful symptoms that accompany it all seem part of the joy and therefore easy to bear.

She also knows that in a little while her reactions will settle down and that even if she has had "quite a turn," it will soon pass. So she waits contentedly without worrying about its passing, and, of course, the feelings gradually calm. May I remind you again that these feelings of happy stress are the same feelings that come with nervous illness; they differ only in being less severe and in being accompanied by a different emotional tone.

IN PLACE OF HAPPINESS PUT PANIC

In place of a happy incident put an impending visit by a nervously ill woman to the hairdresser, dentist, or a school meeting. Instead of happiness, she feels an inner core of apprehension, even panic, and whereas the happy woman did not worry about her stress symptoms, the nervously ill woman notices her feelings immediately because:

1. They have been coming so consistently for such a long

time that they are triggered to come more acutely than the feelings of stress which accompany the shock of unexpected happiness.

2. They are so well known to the nervously ill person that she anticipates them—even goes looking for them—with a feeling of dread or fear.

3. When one is in a fearful state, thoughts are invariably turned inward, not outward as when in a happy state. The woman therefore becomes even more conscious of what is happening within herself than of outside events. Palpitations are always unpleasant, but do they really upset when the heart palpitates for joy? Consider that.

AN ORDINARY DAY IN A NERVOUSLY ILL HOUSEWIFE'S LIFE

Since the majority of my patients have been housewives who are alone all day (how little some husbands understand what this means), perhaps with one or two children dragging at their skirts, I will describe the day of a nervously ill housewife and show how she holds back her own recovery by trying to completely rid herself of her reactions. Do not think I have forgotten the lonely spinster or bachelor or the married man who struggles to work each day. Fundamentally, they will find their situation and their reactions are not so different from those of the housewife. At least, it will not be difficult for them to substitute their situation for hers and to apply my explanation to themselves.

Waking Up

When she first wakes in the morning, realization that another day is here to be faced may strike the sick housewife before she even opens her eyes. This thought immediately brings anguish, and anguish reawakens the symptoms of stress. Then as she wakens further and remembers more vividly some threatening duty of the day—perhaps a school function at night or Wednesday's heavy midweek shopping—more spasms of anguish follow, one after the other, so the sensations she dreads finally merge into one long inner churning. To her this is a very disappointing start to the day and a very tiring one.

After further panic, with her resistance already lowered by months or years of suffering, she may feel exhausted and then depressed. What little store of energy she has gained from her night's rest is almost depleted by nervous reaction to her own thoughts before she even tries to get herself out of bed. Her limbs seem so leaden she may feel incapable of moving them. Necessity eventually forces her up, however, and she finally "points the body" (as one woman put it) at the day's work.

Now she is fumbling under the bed for her slippers. The very repetition of stooping and groping under the bed and then forcing her foot past that faded nylon pompon brings back the memory of the countless mornings she has done the very same thing, feeling exactly as she does now. Memory, what misery you can bring when we let ourselves be ridden by you! Unhappy memory and despair are cousins, so this housewife sighs deeply in despair as she struggles into her dressing gown. Trapped by memory, her thoughts become all despair, and since her body is at the mercy of her thoughts, what else could it do but feel "worse than ever"! *She has already made memory part of the day's burden*—a big mistake.

She used not to feel like this. Indeed, she may have been active and most capable. Feeling this way is so unlike her old self. It seems as if she is two people, one moving in a dream, the other getting breakfast. She feels unreal.

The Sudden Silence Seems Overpowering

When the noise of the family's departure is abruptly stilled by the final closure of the front door, the sudden silence seems more overpowering than the noise had been.

At least the noise meant someone was there—a prop to divert her attention. Now all that attention is directed toward herself, and the last thing she wants is to have her mind on herself, on her illness. And yet she knows this is exactly what she will have, probably for the whole day. There seems no way out for her. Her heart quails at the thought. Whose wouldn't? More anguish. So she pours herself a cup of coffee before facing the stack of dishes in the sink; and while she drinks, she thinks how hopeless it all is, how futile to imagine she could possibly recover, when she can hardly find the strength or courage to face *one* day.

Is it any wonder she feels defeated? Look at the circle in which she has been turning, almost like the blindfolded ass that drags the millstone round and round to grind the corn. Look at the circle. Memory of past suffering and the anticipated suffering of the day ahead bring despair. . . . Despair brings stress. . . . Stress brings even more acutely sensitized feelings . . . which lead to more despair; and the cycle continues, back to more stress and so on.

What a pattern! And this pattern is repeated in so many of the day's activities. Consider the shopping. This housewife may not leave the house to go shopping until midmorning, and between waking and setting off, she gives herself little spurts of panic whenever she thinks of the outing to come. Two hours of intermittent panic would weaken even a strong man, so by the time midmorning comes, her legs already feel weak and wobbly, and she feels lightheaded, giddy. She is not surprised by this. She has been expecting and dreading it. It is one of the reasons why she doesn't want to go out alone. She thinks it is part of her illness, and to avoid feeling this way while out, she would rather not go. She had hoped today might be different, but once again she thinks she will be forced to send the children to do the shopping when they return from school.

At the thought of school, her heart misses a beat—the

school meeting that evening! She had forgotten about that! How will she make *that* when she feels so weak already? More anguish. And what if they ask her to look at the children's paintings in the crowded, hot classroom! That would be the end! School function? Heavens! That means half an hour under the drier at the hairdresser's. She had forgotten that one too! Anguish, more anguish.

So there she is. To every situation—and yet such ordinary situations—she reacts with panic, and her body dutifully and naturally answers with more stress symptoms. She does not understand that these are not sick reactions —but that the sickness lies in their exaggeration, not in their actual occurrence.

"Will I? Won't I?"

When she thinks of disappointing the family once more, she feels lost. So one minute she decides to go, the next minute she cannot face the thought of it. After an hour or so of "Will I? Won't I? Can I? Can't I?" the tension of indecision brings on agitation; agitation makes her tremble, and when this starts, she feels utterly defeated.

The sad part of all this is she has defeated herself. The feelings she dreads most are intense simply because months, even years, of fear have made them so. For example, her fear of the weakness uses up extra glucose, and this creates more weakness. Her fear of panic produces more adrenalin, which excites her nerves to produce more panic. She is not a doctor, though, and does not understand these reactions. So she stays blindly afraid, blindly weak, blindly at home. Once more she thinks her body is doing this to her. So it is, but merely by responding in a physiologically correct way to the fears she brings it.

The Physiology of Nervous Weakness

Let me explain the physiology of nervous weakness. To provide energy for movement our body burns glucose in our muscle cells. Glucose is also burned for energy to express emotion—fear, anger, even joy. This glucose circulates in our blood. When we use up available supplies of glucose too quickly with too much emotion, there may not be enough to provide energy for normal movement. Although we can still move, we feel weak and shaky. Also, the adrenaline released by stress dilates blood vessels in our muscles, so that blood drains from our body into our legs, adding to our feeling of weakness. If we wait as calmly as possible, our liver will break down its stored glycogen into glucose and liberate this extra supply. In addition, the blood vessels gradually recover their tone, and blood circulates normally.

Does this woman wait patiently, though, even as patiently as her "nerves" will let her? Not she. She becomes even more agitated by the weakness and so burns up much of the extra glucose as quickly as her liver supplies it. Naturally the weakness takes unnecessarily long to pass.

Of course, it is the thought of what might happen while out that is helping to bring the panic. What could happen outside is only a repetition of what has been happening at home since early morning. She has already gone a long way toward suffering as intensely as she could away from home, but she does not realize it.

How Can She Face the Drier at the Hairdresser's?

In place of weakness she may feel such stiffness in her legs that they seem difficult to move. This stiffness—sometimes almost a feeling of paralysis—is no more than muscular contraction, a body's normal response to excessive tension. Neck muscles may also be tense and aching; in her words, her neck "feels awful." Agitation makes her heart race, her face flush; she feels burning "all over," as if she "will burst." Feeling this way, how can she face the drier at the hairdresser's? How will she manage to sit there, "chained" for half an hour? More panic. And yet for the sake of a family that cannot possibly measure her sacrifice, this woman may battle into the salon to face a hell her own fears have created in her sensitized body.

Surely these are reasonable fears. None of these experiences is nice to have. Anyone would want to withdraw from them. Yet they are all normal reactions under the circumstances, and to recover *she must not hope to abolish them* but to reduce their intensity. This is the only answer.

She Dreams the Impossible Dream

Let us return to that early morning awakening and see how she can be helped. If she expects to wake feeling well at this stage in her illness, she dreams the impossible dream. One night's sleep will not work that miracle. Yet this is exactly what she does expect. Each night when she lays her head on the pillow, she prays for just that—to wake up feeling her old self. Before she even goes to sleep, her very hopes are preparing the way for disappointment the next day; so when she wakens and feels as ill as ever, of course her body registers anguish. It is only reacting naturally to her disappointment. Her body is her servant; it follows her directions, although she may not even put into words what she thinks, may not even think clearly. She may simply feel misery, and then an overwhelming flood of disappointment follows—disappointment that was inevitable while her body is as sensitized as it is. Knowing the facts about sensitization as we now know them, surely it is easy to see that her overwhelming flood of disappointment was wasted emotion and an unnecessary drain on her limited resources of strength.

If one could only whisper in her ear at night: "Do not be disappointed however you feel in the morning. Please do not add despair and exhaust yourself still further. Just for once be prepared to take yourself as you find yourself, without being so upset because you are as you are. Do not knock your head against the brick wall of despair. Play along with it tomorrow to the best of your ability. Try not to expect the impossible now; you will be like this for a while yet, so if you must point the body, point it willingly. When you go to bed, do not pray to wake feeling well. *Pray to wake with the courage to accept yourself as you find yourself in the morning.*"

Breaking the Chain of Memory

When she fumbles under the bed for her slippers, she needs special help. She should buy new slippers for a start—if possible, rather foolish ones that make her smile, but at least a new pair. She might try to remember to put them somewhere else, not under the bed every night. Breaking the chain of memory even in such foolish little ways as this helps. It breaks the repetition of moments of suffering, so that she does not think despairingly so readily. When she thinks despairingly, she immediately *feels* despair. This is a natural reaction in her state. So many of her early morning reactions are to be expected under the circumstances. As already mentioned, *it is the exaggeration in the feeling of despair, the exaggeration in her body's responses, that is the sickness*. To help herself further she could change the position of the furniture in her room, especially the bed, so on waking she does not see the same familiar pattern of things—that special spot on the ceiling—to remind her of the many other mornings of identical suffering.

"Even If My Legs Go Weak, They Can Still Carry Me!"

If only she would give herself a chance during those hours of waiting to go shopipng and say to herself, "If I keep frightening myself, of course my legs will feel weak and I'll feel giddy. That's only natural, and it is not an illness. Even if my legs go weak, they can still carry me when I go out. So I'll try to walk as calmly as I can manage, however I feel. If my legs can carry me home after I've been panicking, surely they can carry me forward in between panics. If I do this as willingly as I can, my liver will supply more glucose, and the weakness will gradually pass!"

At last she would be giving her body a chance. And if only she would then continue by saying, "Of course I'll feel awful at the hairdresser's. I've been feeling awful there for so long that I'm not going to stop now just because I want to! I may make great strides doing other things— like going on a vacation—and still find the hairdresser's just as difficult, perhaps worse, when I come home. This doesn't mean I am sick again. It only means memory is up to its old tricks. I will probably have to sit through the hour at the hairdresser's many times thinking the right way before I no longer dread going there!"

You who are suffering and read this, turn your attention to the way you think, not to your feelings. Come to terms with your attitude, and your feelings will look after themselves.

TWO KINDS OF SUFFERERS

I wish to mention two different kinds of sufferers. One says, "I can't help any of it coming. It just comes. I'm not doing it to myself. I suddenly feel dreadful when I'm not even thinking about my illness. That is what is so hard to understand."

The other says, "I know I am doing this to myself, but I feel powerless to stop it. That is what is so terrible!"

"I Can't Help Any of It Coming!"

Consider the first person. There are indeed times when some nervous symptoms do seem to strike for no special reason and appear to be unrelated to the sufferer's occupation at that particular moment; however, they are a result of what he has done to himself in the past. Past suffering has prepared nervous reactions to come so swiftly and easily that the slightest stimulus, perhaps unrecognized by him and certainly beyond his direct control, may bring them. It is in his power, however, to gradually soothe this hyper-irritability by accepting these "out of the blue" attacks and by not being continually surprised and upset by them.

"I Am Doing This to Myself!"

The person who says he knows he is frightening himself and is powerless to stop it must try to understand that this is only a natural outcome of his body's instant response to his slightest thought. As I have pointed out before, in a sensitized person, feeling—especially fear—follows thought so closely that not only do they both often seem as one, but also it seems sometimes as if there is no thought —only feeling. This in itself is confusing and hard to bear, so the nervous person sometimes stays frightened, although there is no outside cause for his fear. Naturally, he thinks he is frightening himself, and in a sense he is. His aim should be to reduce the intensity and speed of his responses so that reason can come into the picture. To do this he must try to look ahead and not stay emotionally bound to each minute of the day. He needs a long-range program. Let him say to himself, "I've been frightening myself for a long time, so I'll probably go on doing it while my feelings respond so quickly to what I am thinking. If I understand this is because I am sensitized and if I try not to be too upset by it, then perhaps in a little while fear may not flash so quickly." I can assure him that if he does this, he will eventually be able to think calmly even of fear itself—without frightening himself.

If I could only give all of you the courage to put my teaching into practice—not to look for a cure in new drugs, a new cause, but to go out prepared to take what comes without tensely steeling yourself against it—then I would indeed be leading you to recovery.

There is still so much to say. I know that some of you —the mother of six, for example—are so weary, so sensitized, that you need practical help, not just words alone. You need some sedation and rest for a little while, perhaps a tonic, before trying to practice my teaching.

If like this, why not discuss your situation with an understanding doctor, pointing out to him that as soon as you feel better, you have a positive plan for recovery? Unfortunately some healthy young doctors do not understand how desperately weary some of you are—how could they? If they see you are determinedly armed with a blueprint for recovery, however, their interest will be aroused, and I am sure they will help you to improve your physical health.

So:

- Recovery lies in reducing nervous symptoms to normal intensity and normal frequency, not in trying to abolish them entirely.
- No one can completely banish *normal* reactions, and nervous reactions are no more than normal reactions exaggerated.
- Try not to make memory part of the day's burden.
- One night's sleep will not work a miracle.
- Try to accept yourself as you find yourself in the morning.
- Point the body willingly.

JOURNAL 2: Program for Recovery, Tranquilization, Special Fears

Some of you who are afraid to travel away from home, either alone or with others, have come to a standstill after your first successful efforts. So I begin this journal with a talk on the kind of setback you may be now experiencing.

It is an advantage for a nervously ill person to work away from home, and I know from your letters many of you who go out to work are now not only moving more freely than you have for a long time but are also less anxious when at work. There remain the many hundreds of sufferers whose work is at home—work that does not automatically provide opportunity to practice my teaching. They must make their own opportunities, and these are the people who may now be needing special direction and help.

When they first used my book and records, and later the journal, they may have started off with enthusiasm and hope and may have accomplished feats not attempted for years—such as walking to the end of the street, then as far as the shops, perhaps later entering a shop and even standing in a line. When they did this, they may have thought they had conquered the world; at the least they had a feeling of making progress, of getting somewhere at last. Now they are faced with the thought "Where do I go from there? What do I do next?" It is as if they have come to a dead stop and have begun to wonder if they have achieved anything at all.

These people are at a standstill because what they can do now—at least, without too much difficulty—has become so much part of their everyday life—that the *doing* no longer seems an event. More important still, at the back of their minds lurks the thought that to be really cured they must move *further afield*. They know recovery now lies along the rougher roads, and they balk at the thought. They stay hemmed in by their short walks, their small endeavors, and feel they need a gigantic thrust from somewhere to make them take off along that distant threatening but beckoning way. At the same time, they dread being given that thrust. They both desire and dread simultaneously—an unsettling feeling in itself and enough to keep tension alive.

The person who works away from home is rarely alone. He is with people during the day, even when traveling to work, and is usually with the family in the evening. The diversion company brings relieves introspection and helps keep troubles in proportion. The person who need not leave home daily soon has to face the fact that she must rely on herself to plan her own program of recovery —one that takes her out of the house. She will also find that although the small goals are near at hand, reaching the bigger ones may mean taking journeys that seem not only impossible but also—and this is so important—pointless. There is little inspiration in taking a bus to such-and-such a place and then simply taking another bus home. To go in cold blood? Just there and back? That is asking a lot, especially on cold, dull days, when home fires are so cozy. This aimlessness of their road to recovery may make such people feel even more aware of their illness as something unusual and hopeless—especially hopeless after having tasted the joy, the promises, the hopes, those early successes brought. This is why so many get stuck at this point. Remember, though, that if you are like this, bogged down though you may seem, *you have begun to recover.* Any early success is a beginning and once made can never be quite lost or forgotten, however far down the ladder you may think you have slipped.

If there is a family cheering from the sidelines, the adventurer can at least announce later in the day she went to such-and-such a place or did such-and-such a thing. Even these lucky people, however, have to go through the deflated feeling of returning to an empty house immediately after their big endeavor and waiting until evening to break the good news. This is difficult enough, but how much more difficult it is for the person with an uninterested family or with no family at all. I would like such people reading this journal to take special encouragement.

I recently had the following conversation with a woman which highlights some of the points just made:

PATIENT: I have improved my walking down the street by about twenty yards, but that seems to be my limit. Last week there was one day when I couldn't even do that, so I went as far as I could and then came back and waited half an hour and went out again in the opposite direction. I actually entered a shop and bought something. Now I can do that quite easily, so I think, "Where do I go from there?"

DOCTOR: Yes. These efforts begin to seem purposeless.

PATIENT: And it seems just as hard as ever to go beyond the boundary I set for myself!

DOCTOR: What is your next boundary beyond that one?

PATIENT: The town center. I'm trying to walk there because I will be surrounded by shops. It is only another hundred yards farther, but I can't seem to make it. I can't get beyond the first twenty yards.

DOCTOR: You are making the mistake of trying to cope with the distance, of trying to get as far as the town center. You all make the same mistake; you fix your eyes on a distant point and try to urge yourself toward it, thinking "I *must* get there. I *must* make it!" Do not do it that way. *It is yourself you have to cope with,* not a certain distance or a special place. It is coping with yourself that matters, not "making" the town center. It is coping with *that one moment, the moment of extreme panic*—wherever you might be—that is important. When you go through any journey, whether it is only a few yards from home or on towards the town center (or even staying at home alone), I want you to understand that the worst you have to go through is *that one moment.* Even when you are in the town center, surrounded by shops and people, surrounded by the *worst* that can frighten you, it is still *only the same moment* you have to face. It is never very different. Never forget that! So please try not to be deterred by any threatening future event that may seem especially frightening. The very worst experience can bring you only *that same moment. Learn how to cope with it, and you will have coped with everything.* I have explained how to cope with the moment of panic again and again in my book and records.

PATIENT: Yes, you have, and I know I did cope with it going up the street for those twenty yards, but going into the town seems different.

DOCTOR: This is because you put a set objective and strain toward it. Do not strain toward anything. Go moment by moment if necessary, and say to yourself, "I'm practicing going toward the town center. If I don't get there, it doesn't matter. What matters is that I learn how to cope with the feelings that arise within me as I go along." How *far* you go is not important: *How* you go is the important thing.

PATIENT: But the further I go, the more panics I'll have to cope with, and it is so exhausting; and if I get a long way from home, the panics will be awful, and I'll still have to get back home!

DOCTOR: Getting back home will not be so difficult. A homing pigeon has nothing on you.

PATIENT: You are right. But what about all the panics that come as I get further and further away from home?

DOCTOR: You cope with each exactly as you coped with the one before it, by going toward it and not shrinking from it. You use the same recipe for each. Go slowly, wait, and let the panic flash and spend itself. Sometimes it may seem to never quite die down and may smolder on all the time you are out. You can still function with this inner smoldering. Do not be bluffed by this. It is only sensitized nerves *recovering* from the blasts you have just given them and quivering under the little blasts you continue to give them. I know you think you lose control of yourself during a real "scorcher" and believe you cannot think. You can think, all right! You can think very clearly, "This is the end! This is it! Now I know I'm going to die. I'll have to get home quickly!" When you flash in this way, I want you to think just two words —utter acceptance. By utter acceptance I mean let your body go as loose as you can, pass through the flash, and then go on with what you are doing. If you are driving a car, you may have to pull over to the side for a while before you go on, but then *go on*.

PATIENT: I'm not likely to be driving a car! But I know what you mean.

DOCTOR: I hope you do because when you do it this way, you eventually reach a stage where you feel you could go on for miles. When you come through the worst and understand how you did it, the long journey unfolds before you as something you can cope with—because it can bring you nothing you have not already been through successfully. It no longer seems like a brick wall against which you are trying to hurl yourself. *The long journey unfolds.*

PATIENT: Oh dear! I know what you say is right. But can *I* do it? That's the point!

DOCTOR: Your body functions the same as the body of any other person, so why shouldn't you be able to? Treat it as I have advised, and it must respond as any other body would. There is no special set of physiological rules for you. I am not asking you to rely on me but on the fundamental laws of physiology.

PATIENT: What is physiology?

DOCTOR: It is the study of how a body functions. There is no such thing as Doctor Weekes's method. I teach nature's method. I am showing you what nature will do if you give her a chance.

PATIENT: I don't like nature one little bit!

DOCTOR: Of course you don't, the way you misuse her. I have a suggestion to make. Start off *toward* the town center this morning, and don't turn back until you have tried to go through one "blaster" with utter acceptance.

PATIENT: I'll try.

DOCTOR: Don't be disappointed if you fail the first time. The important thing is that you are willing to try. If you fail, wait *where you are* and try again. Don't turn quickly and run home.

PATIENT: I think if I had a chance to stay out long enough, I could go right through this, and then I would be able to carry on and get some feeling of achievement, which I find so hard to get now. I would be able to measure what I had done. I know I have made improvement,

Doctor, but I am still only aware of my limitations. So many of us rush and we are back too quickly to an empty house and we feel let down and frustrated because it seems such a little thing to have done—and we still have the day to get through. We can't keep trying, because it makes us so tired. Speaking of tiredness, I do feel terribly tired. I am going out to dinner tonight; I have accepted that I am going, and I am going, but I feel *so* tired. Before, when I forced myself, I didn't seem to get so tired. Why is this?

DOCTOR: With acceptance comes a certain "letting go." One can nurse a sick parent for weeks without feeling particularly tired while the need is there, but when the danger is over, we may "go to pieces." Acceptance is rather like that. It means a giving in, and with giving in comes a slackening. This is excellent for desensitization, but until your body recovers its tone, whatever relaxation you have achieved may seem like extra weariness. In time this passes.

PROGRAM FOR RECOVERY

This woman will now practice going toward the town center. What of those who have no town center so conveniently placed within walking distance? If you are like this, you must draw up a plan of action to suit your own locality. Plan two days ahead and then a day's break. Do not wait until Monday to begin; this will give you too much time to work yourself "into a state." Start this afternoon if possible; also include part of each weekend in your practice. If after two days' effort and one day's rest, you feel especially tired, give yourself a longer rest. In the beginning when you first go out practicing, you so often naturally do it the wrong way from habit that you become resensitized and are more easily fatigued. Hence you may need extra tranquilization at this stage. I discuss this later in this bulletin. Do not wait too long, wondering whether you are refreshed enough to practice once more. It is surprising how success refreshes and how failure tires. So do not wait too long in failure. Use your common sense.

WALK AS FAR AS THE NEAREST BUS STOP

Your plan should start with something a little more difficult than you have already tried. For example, if you have not been in a bus on your own, I suggest your first effort should be to walk as far as the nearest bus stop. If the stop is too close, walk to the stop farther on. If it is too far, walk half the distance. At least walk in the direction of the stop.

If you manage to reach it, time your walk so that you will arrive there *when a bus is due*. If you can do only this much until you receive the next journal, it will have been a good deal to have done. Once you have made your plan, *stick to it*. It is so easy to postpone going out if it is raining or if you tell yourself you do not feel up to it. If you put off going, make sure you have a good reason.

Because I have asked you to walk only *as far as* the bus stop, do not think I am discouraging you from boarding the bus. If it comes while you are there and you feel prompted to take it, do so. Go to the next group of shops. Have in mind that one day you might suddenly find yourself in a bus, so plan now how far you would go. This will save some confusion on that great occasion. Please don't feel compelled to board a bus at this stage, however. It is enough to practice walking to the bus stop, *coping the right way* with those moments of panic, those "jelly legs," and that faint feeling.

"I WOULD RATHER THE PANIC CAME TO GET IT OVER WITH!"

When you have truly learned how to cope with panic, fear of it will gradually grow less; and as fear goes, so do "jelly legs" and faint feelings. This may bring its own strangeness. One woman said, "When I do things now without the usual panic, it all seems so quiet, strange—awfully peculiar. It is as if there is some kind of silent monster waiting to pounce. I would almost rather panic and get it over with. At least I would feel alive!"

Recovery can be strange. The newness of successfully doing the ordinary everyday things that previously frightened you may make you feel so unreal that you become apprehensive of recovery. Accept even this, and realize others besides you feel this same strangeness.

MAKE THE MOST OF ANY RESPITE

You need repeated practice at accepting until you have truly learned your lesson. Your inner core of certainty comes only from repeated doing—and in the beginning from "repeated doing" at fairly frequent intervals, as suggested earlier in this journal. Do not let too many days elapse between efforts, but do not force yourself if you have been trying very hard and suddenly feel tired, flat, and dispirited; wait a few days—even a few weeks if necessary—until your spirits revive. It is so difficult to distinguish between real fatigue and only thinking you are tired, isn't it? And it is difficult to know when you should go on and when you should ease up. The important thing is that once you decide to rest, do not fret because you are doing nothing about your problem for the moment. Make the most of any respite.

ALL THE LITTLE THINGS REMIND YOU OF OTHER OCCASIONS

When you have been practicing the right way, even if much time elapses between practices, you will find that although the contemplation of doing may still make action seem as difficult as ever, once you start moving, the memory of your previous successes will help you. For example, if you have already made successful bus journeys and have temporarily reverted to dread of making another, you will find once you are in a bus that all the little things that go with being in a bus remind you of the other occasions when you managed successfully; and your inner core of confidence will gradually come to life again, even if shakily at first.

No success, however small, is ever completely lost while you recover the way I teach you. It is the hard way, yes, but this is why you make your success part of yourself. You earn it. Setbacks may come, but even these will gradually pass if you originally worked your way through your illness by your own effort. After the first shock of setback courage will return. This may take some time because you are indeed shocked by it—shocked to think it could happen to you just when you thought you were so well, especially shocked at meeting so many of the old symptoms you hoped you had lost forever. *Let the first shock pass.*

I mentioned courage. Recovery is not built on knowing you had the courage to board the bus and sit through hell with clenched teeth. This wearies and discourages. Recovery lies in learning to sit in the bus with the right attitude. It lies in sitting there with utter acceptance of anything your body may seem to do to you and, more important, *of anything you may think and so do to yourself.*

TRANQUILIZATION

I am assuming your doctor is regulating any tranquilization you are having. I make one suggestion: If you contemplate some big effort—such as a social gathering, a long journey—and find you build up much tension the night before (or the days before), extra sedation at this time is helpful, but first discuss this with your doctor. In time, with repeated "doing," you will anticipate less acutely, and extra sedation will not be necessary. Also, it may be a good idea to discuss with your doctor the advisability of having a little added tranquilization during your early efforts to recover, when sensitization is likely to increase a little. I do not mean you should take additional tablets continuously but only on those days when you are especially sensitized. Also, any extra dose should not be enough to make you lethargic. You need your doctor's help with this problem. He knows the dosage you are now on; he also knows you and whether you are likely to become dependent on the extra amount.

SPECIAL FEARS

Since writing to you I have read in detail the many requests from you for journals. The fears you have mentioned are the same fears my own patients have so often described. They are the fears most people have at some time or other, although perhaps not as acutely as you now have them. Which of us has not felt at least some of these: fear of being alone, of loneliness, of feeling inadequate, of ill health, of dying, of going insane, of fainting, of thunderstorms, of some animal—spiders, cats, and so on—of not recovering from illness, of harming others while "like this," of "ending it all"? None of these fears is individual. As I said, most non–nervously ill people feel some of them at some time but take them as a matter of course. We took them upon ourselves when we chose to be human and not just animals lying in the sun. They are part of our existence, and their nature does not necessarily make them part of a neurosis. They are very human fears.

The nervously ill, sensitized person is at a disadvantage because he feels his fears so acutely; they are magnified.

Sometimes when he is particularly tense or agitated, a special fear may strike mind and heart so suddenly and with such compelling force that it feels as if he is assailed by a power outside himself.

REDUCING THE INTENSITY OF FEAR

People who are not nervously ill are able to keep their fears in perspective. Their reactions are not severe, so they can place the fears beside the joys of ordinary living, and in this way the fears play only a small part in their lives. The nervously ill person's fea s, however, may be so strong that they spoil his life and may be so constantly with him that they can mar any so-called happy occasion.

As with the symptoms of stress, it is the intensity, not the nature of the fear, that so often matters; and to recover one must reduce one's fears to normal intensity. One cannot hope to be rid entirely of all fears. I have yet to meet the person who has no special fear in the background, but this is the point: They are able to keep their fears *in the background, in proportion*.

There are several ways of reducing the intensity of fear. Firstly, the fear can be discussed with a wise counselor (doctor, religious adviser, friend) who may help the sufferer to see his fears from a reasonable point of view. He may need many discussions at frequent intervals before he can see reason and draw comfort from it. This is where a doctor's tape recording of an interview is especially helpful for a patient; it can be played many times daily if needed. *It is possible to adjust oneself eventually to special fears and live happily in spite of them.*

Secondly, after discussion and after being given a new approach to understanding a particular fear, the sufferer must be prepared for the time being to continue to react acutely when he thinks of his fear. He must learn to pass through each fear flash and go on quietly with whatever he might be doing, at the same time practicing seeing his fear from the new approach his counselor (or maybe these journals) has given him. With practice, the fear gradually lessens, so that eventually he keeps a continuity of interest in his work even as fear strikes. When fear no longer hinders, it gradually loses importance.

Desensitization to a special fear takes time and patience. I call this approach glimpsing. Glimpsing works, but it is not easy, and one must persevere for success.

It is comforting for a sufferer to know that many people share his fears and that they have managed to keep them within bearable limits. If they can, why not he?

WHAT CAUSES FEARS?

One could argue that some special fear makes a person ill, and so one has only to find the cause of the fear, remove it, and the sufferer will recover. That sounds logical, and it often succeeds. Others say that if you remove one fear, the sufferer will soon find another to take its place, and that some may even be using their fears as an escape from facing reality. There is so much speculation when discussing nervous illness. Each doctor can speak with authority only from his experience with his own patients. In my practice, to the best of my understanding, I have found that although some patients recover when the cause of a special fear is removed, many had originally been sensitized, as I have explained in my book and records (by shock, accident, operation, difficult confinement, domestic upsets, and so on); and while in this sensitized state one or more of their dormant fears—the ordinary human fears we have been talking about—suddenly brought such exaggerated reaction that it became alive with importance and leapt straight to the center of the stage. Also, any new fear such a sensitized person may feel may acquire magnified significance. Indeed, because of his sensitization, he now finds fear in corners where before he found none. This is sometimes called free-floating anxiety.

To put it another way, isn't it understandable that if a sensitized person were able to dispel one fear, his sensitization would soon exaggerate another of his dormant fears? A sensitized person does not necessarily seek these fears for himself. They are already there. *His newly acquired sensitization vitalizes and magnifies them into importance.* I find my patients only too anxious to be rid of their fears and get on with their life. Of course, there are always the old chronic work-dodgers, but I am not concerned with them here. I am concerned with people who are willing to try to recover. You are the kind of people I am accustomed to treating—the people I have grown to respect, *whatever your fears, setbacks, failures.* I wish you all the courage to have another try.

So:

- Recovery can seem strange. Accept even this.
- Make the most of every respite.
- No success, however small, is completely lost.
- Let the first shock pass.
- Recovery lies in establishing the right attitude.
- Relax with each fear flash; let it pass, and at the same time practice glimpsing your fear from the right point of view.

JOURNAL 3: Right-Reaction Readiness, Reacting Freely, Gaining Confidence, Going on Vacation

RIGHT-REACTION READINESS

Some of you have succeeded in walking as far as the bus stop; others have actually traveled by bus. Some have even made train journeys alone. Others have returned to work for the first time in years. These efforts are excellent; however, I hope you will understand that I am still concerned with those who have not yet found the courage to board a vehicle or face any other dreaded situation, whatever it might be.

Therefore I now suggest a special exercise in our program of recovery. It is called right-reaction readiness, and you can practice it at home. Right-reaction readiness will help you not only to begin moving or to face any other special difficulty but also to shorten the time of recovery itself.

By right-reaction readiness I mean one has prepared oneself to meet stressful situations the right way so often that the right approach is established as a habit; in other words, *the right reaction is ready.*

Those of you who still find achievement difficult do so partly because you remember your past failures and how you felt then so clearly that when you think of going through those experiences again, your reactions are automatically dislike, panic, withdrawal. Unwittingly you are in a state of wrong-reaction readiness. Indeed, as far as wrong-reaction readiness is concerned, you are in the front line of performers.

I hasten to explain that by right-reaction readiness I do not mean being tensely on guard to react the right way. Do not become caught in that net. I simply mean one gradually establishes the habit of reacting the right way, both by mental preparation (the treatment I will now describe) and by actual performance.

We learn to play tennis by practicing the correct strokes again and again until finally we do them without thinking much about them. When preparing to play a concerto, a performer will practice slowly and pay great attention to detail and technique; the more he practices in this way, the more groundwork he will have to depend on when he is actually on the platform waiting for the conductor to raise the baton. The more ground he has prepared, the more easily he will be able to rise above making the effort of physical performance and give a free, inspiring interpretation; but the physical preparation must be thorough before he can forget the effort. By diligent practice he has laid down the necessary association pathways to bring him the right reaction automatically. Are you beginning to understand what I mean by right-reaction readiness? Let me illustrate this again by recording part of a conversation I had with a patient. He said, "When I mentioned being on guard some weeks ago, I know now I was on guard watching to stop myself 'listening in' and bringing on a 'turn.' I should have been on guard ready to relax and accept anything which might come. It's not like that now. I've learned how to see a turn through, without reaching for the pill bottle. I can even work with the panic there. I'm not saying I don't mind it—I do; it's still horrible—but it doesn't throw me the way it did. I've learned what you mean by 'letting go.' " At last he had the right reaction—relaxation with acceptance—and most important, he had it ready.

This brings us to the crux of the matter: how to make right-reaction readiness a habit. You can practice the following plan just as you would practice anything else.

THE IMAGINARY BUS APPROACHES

Sit in a comfortable chair and imagine you are in one of the situations, any demanding situation, you fear most —for example, if agoraphobic, that you are about to take your first bus ride alone. While sitting in your chair, relax to the best of your ability, and then imagine yourself in this situation. Let us suppose you are at the bus stop, waiting for the bus. As the imaginary bus approaches, try to feel the same misgivings and fears you would feel if you were really there. Try to make your reactions as real and as severe as you can. As you experience them, remain as relaxed as possible and think, "What would Doctor Weekes advise me to do now?" Try to remember my advice, and practice *feeling* yourself following it. Of course, I would want you to let the fears come and to be prepared to meet the bus *with the fear there,* to wobble on "jelly legs" if necessary but to still direct them toward the bus, to let the panic come and not to be deterred by any weakness that may follow: in other words, to accept the whole "box of tricks" and *move forward* with acceptance.

REACTING FREELY

You may be so tired of hearing the word "accept" that I will use another expression and tell you to move forward, prepared to "react freely." By that I mean give free rein to all feelings; do not try to put a brake on any of them; let them all come. Do not fear that by doing this the feelings will be so overpowering they will immobilize you. The "freely" saves you, cures you eventually, because it releases enough tension to encourage action.

It is possible that the term "reacting freely" (or "free reaction") may help some of you more than the word "acceptance." Different words, different phrases, have different effects on different people, and "reacting freely" is a good term. It describes well what I mean.

So I would like you to sit in your chair and visualize the scene of boarding the bus, at the same time having the courage to try to feel yourself reacting freely. Having mounted the bus, look for a seat at the front (not near the door in this bus!); even imagine yourself groping for your fare and hearing the bus driver make some disparaging remark like, "Come on, lady, I don't have all day. Can't you move a little faster?" Which, of course, is just what you can't do.

When in your seat remind yourself you cannot leave

the bus in a hurry. Go through any emergency you can conjure up—even to the bus breaking down and your having to change buses—and as you feel fear, try to remember what I would advise you to do. Say it aloud, and try to *feel* this right reaction. The key to this practicing is to remain as relaxed as possible while you imagine each situation you fear. The more you practice, even if only in imagination, the more readily the right reaction will come when you find yourself actually in the situation. Indeed, after practicing like this, you will sooner or later find yourself in a bus or train or driving your car or facing up to any other situation you have previously avoided. Do not be afraid to fail at this practice, but if you do, search for the reason, admit it, and try again.

BEHAVIORISM

Some of you may think the practice I have suggested is an application of behaviorism. Right-reaction readiness differs from behaviorism in at least one fundamental. Behaviorism, with or without the help of drugs, aims at removing the fear associated with certain thoughts or experiences. Right-reaction readiness trains you by taking you through fear, not by avoiding it or trying to switch it off. The patient treated by behaviorism who has not learned how to pass through fear may find fear lurking in the shadows, ready to come forward in the future, perhaps in some new guise. There is only one way to reduce fear to bearable intensity without drugs, and that is by learning how to cope with it at its worst, not by trying to avoid it.

FEAR-REMOVING DRUGS

That is also my answer to those who have written for my advice on taking certain recently publicized "fear-removing" drugs. Drugs have a limited time of action, so one must either continue taking them, hoping they do not lose their effect and have no harmful side effects, or one must sooner or later wean oneself from them. When weaning time comes, imagination can flash doubt in a second. The person trying to do without the drugs has only to think, "What if I can't manage without them!" to panic and perhaps undo months of progress previously made with the help of medication.

THE ONLY WAY OUT OF FEAR IS THROUGH IT

There is only one way out of our fears, and that is through them. Fear must eventually hold no fear, and it can do this only when we know how to quench its fire by losing fear of the fire itself. Free reaction will, with practice, lead to right-reaction readiness, and the two together will eventually lead to recovery. Start practicing now, at home in your chair.

"I CAN'T FREEWHEEL QUICKLY ENOUGH!"

One woman wrote, "I can't remember your advice quickly enough to freewheel past panic and other nervous feelings." The practice I have just recommended will surely help her, but I would rather she were not so anxious to "freewheel past" panic. This is too much like trying to switch panic off. Because of such intense, well-established wrong-reaction readiness, this woman asks of herself a physiological impossibility at the moment.

This is why I have persistently advised you to find the courage to react freely and take what comes rather than try to avoid it—"freewheel past it." Panic will cease to come of its own accord only when it and other nervous feelings switch themselves off because their coming is no longer significant. This will happen only when you have learned to ride through them so often in the right way that deep within yourself you know that even if they come, they will no longer overwhelm you. When true avoidance comes automatically in this way, from practice and more practice and *not only* in your armchair, you will not have to struggle desperately to remember my advice so that you can "freewheel" past your feelings; the feelings will dissipate themselves.

So:

- Practice free reaction.
- The only way out of fear is through it.

GAINING CONFIDENCE

One man wrote, "If I could feel confidence in myself, I would soon recover. I have very little social life because I am afraid of meeting people. Many of the symptoms described in Chapter 4 of your book *Hope and Help for Your Nerves* have left me or come only on occasion. My chief concern now is loss of confidence. Other people seem so much more confident than I."

First, do not confuse what you think is confidence in others with what could be self-assertiveness. So many apparently self-confident people are merely self-assertive, and they are vulnerable because of this delusion. They have never been put to the test—certainly not to the kind of test you are now meeting. Give them a crisis to meet, and they may find their self-assertiveness of little help. There is no better way to develop real confidence than to come through experiences such as yours. You know how it *feels* to be without confidence, to *feel* almost a nothingness deep within you, so you are at least one step ahead of the self-assertive person who has not had this valuable experience of self-knowledge. At least you are aware of this deficiency in yourself. I do not expect you to appreciate that this awareness is already an achievement, but it is; at least you are not deluding yourself.

I know little about the man who wrote the above letter except that his work brings him into close contact with others who, because of his lack of confidence, I assume show their self-assertiveness in his presence more obviously than they realize, so that coping with them and his work may be a daily battle. He may force himself to meet these people on their own ground and then, after each trying encounter, sink back into himself to face a tiring, even trembling, reaction—natural enough under the circumstances but interpreted by him as further proof of his lack of confidence. Also, this reaction may whittle away at any small feeling of success he may have gained from having exerted himself.

For the moment, this man must be prepared to feel a reaction after any such trying experience, but he should try to understand it is a normal reaction to considerable effort; it is an effort, however, that will gradually grow less when he is ready to accept the way he feels while making it or after having made it. Confidence must come from within oneself, and the price one pays is doing the difficult thing again and again. Successfully accomplishing the difficult once may mean only that at a particular time one had a special spurt of courage. Doing it often means the courage is no longer momentary but has become built in as part of oneself. One *knows* because of *repeated* doing.

No one need add up his failures. Each can be set aside. As I said earlier, *failure is not finality*. It is only as permanent as one will allow it to be. Failure has no will of its own. It hasn't a leg to stand on unless we lend it ours. If you see failure as only a trial that did not succeed one particular time but which may succeed the next time, then failure is no longer failure; it becomes an experience from which much can be learned.

When he finally learns how to face and talk to people by not being too impressed by his feelings of the moment, the writer of that letter will find it will no longer be important whether he *seems* confident or not. Now he not only wants to feel confident, but he also dearly wants to appear confident before others. A truly confident person does not care whether or not he appears confident, does not mind admitting mistakes, does not mind being helped, does not mind asking questions—if they are pertinent. When I finally no longer minded looking up a long-forgotten prescription in front of a patient, I knew I had arrived.

TISSUE-THIN LAYERS

It is as if confidence is laid down in very thin layers —tissue-thin layers—of feeling, day by day, month by month, each layer coming from the experience gained by making some effort, until at last the layers build up into established deep inner feeling. There is no experience more effective in providing those thin layers than the experience you are now passing through. Be glad of this opportunity to acquire real confidence so you need not settle for self-assertiveness, as so many unfortunately do.

The last part of the man's letter shows he is finding the right approach. He says: "If I truly accept myself as I am, I will recover." He will, and what is more, he will find as he accepts himself more willingly that others will accept him more naturally. People will be more at ease with him. The effort will have finally gone.

So:

- What you think is confidence in others may be only self-assertiveness.
- Be prepared to feel a reaction after any trying experience. Do not give it undue importance.
- The price of confidence is doing the difficult thing again and again.
- One *knows* because of repeated doing.
- Failure is not finality. It has no legs to stand on unless we give it ours.
- No experience can bring confidence more effectually than recovery from nervous illness *when it has been won the right way*.

Going on Vacation

How important it is to have an incentive to draw one out of the house. Spring is an incentive. This has been a dreary winter, following last year's disappointingly cold summer. As the warmer, brighter days now beckon you out of doors, you will begin to feel the benefit of my teaching. If you have a bicycle in the garage, prepare it for use. Some of you will think, "How could I ride a bicycle while I am as giddy as this?" If you do it by concentrating on the riding and not on the giddiness, you will find that gradually the giddiness will ease. It is not so difficult to ride with your type of nervous giddiness—the floaty, lightheaded kind. Talk to your doctor if you have not already done so, and get his reassurance your giddiness is nervous. I can only assume it is. I have not examined you.

When you decide to ride—or walk, if you do not cycle—arrange to meet someone, if possible, or make a visit you have not made for a long time. Have the courage to be part of this spring. You can gain it by practicing *free reaction*. The key is in your hands. Use it. Do not be afraid to go out and hear the birds sing and feel the sun shine. It is all yours. Be part of it at last. Look at the flowers, smell them, look at their colors. Enjoy them. All these things are yours. Go to meet them. Do not envy those who go out among them this summer; join them. You can, by quietly practicing everything I have taught you. It works.

SHALL I GO WITH THE FAMILY THIS TIME?

And what of the vacations summer brings? Go, but go understanding vacation can be disappointing for the person trying to recover from nervous illness. Any of us can feel almost incarcerated in a small town or beach resort, and if the weather is bad, the impulse to rush home on the next train can be compelling. Many of you have had this experience and have returned home, dragging the family with you and deciding to never, never, go on vacation again. Or if your husband has held you there against your will, what a miserable vacation it has been. You have counted the hours.

This time, however, you take with you something you have not taken before—an understanding of what to do, a program for taking a vacation. If you can see those first days through, you will find the strange, seemingly inhospitable place will not feel so strange. Indeed, you may find you do not want to leave it at the end of the vacation to return to the old familiar struggle.

A MIND REFRESHED IS A MIND UNCHAINED

To find no struggle at home, one would need to be away much longer than a few weeks—long enough for memory to dull the edge of the fears familiar surroundings can bring. Do not expect your vacation to do great things for you. Be satisfied if you have no more success than seeing the time through.

It could be that you gradually feel freer in those strange streets than you have felt for a long time, and you wonder how this could be while you feel so bound, so restricted, only one block from home. It is very natural. In a new place there are no upsetting memories and much incentive. The streets near home are full of upsetting memories and no incentive. Change refreshes, and a mind refreshed is a mind unchained.

On the other hand, the crowds, the laughter, the fun, may make you feel very aware of your "strangeness," your difference from others. This too is natural. Remember, though, that there may be many in that crowd going through an experience similar to yours. You do not look any different than they do.

THE BUILDUP

When you decide to take the plunge and vacation this summer, the most difficult time will be the great anticipation, the buildup to going, and the first few days after arrival. See these two periods through, and you will be heartened by the results. You may need extra sedation at night, even during the day, at that time. Your doctor should be consulted about this.

While you travel, do not think in terms of distance from home. You take your real home with you—your family and yourself. What you leave behind is a house, dear though it may be. Do not let a house imprison you. Go forward as you travel, and do not leave your mind behind in a house.

RIDE THE FIRST SHOCK

Don't be overawed by the thought "What if something terrible were to happen so far from home?" If you let this thought paralyze you into inactivity, you have already let something terrible happen and *at home*. One can cope away from home *by seeing all moments through without turning them into concrete barriers*. Whatever comes, *ride the first shock*. Take it slowly, and the difficult moment will melt. This is the secret of losing the set-in-cement feeling and regaining flexibility of thought. When you can think more freely, you can move more freely. So go on your vacation this summer, and treat it as another practice session.

AGORAPHOBIA CAN BE CURED

It seems necessary to say definitely once more that agoraphobia can be cured. Please do not be impressed by anything you may read or hear to the contrary. When a person, whoever he may be, says agoraphobia is incurable, he is merely saying he does not know how to cure it. Doctors avoid claiming "cures," but for your sake I am going to brush aside my natural disinclination to do so and tell you positively that I have cured many people of agoraphobia. As an example, some time ago I spoke to a group of agoraphobic women in England. An Australian woman came to the meeting at my invitation. She came alone. When I first saw her, a year earlier in Australia, it was all she could do to make the journey to my office, even with her husband's help. She was cured enough to fly fourteen thousand miles to England and to move freely in London on her own, even by subway. She has now returned home and moves just as freely there. I assure you she is only one of hundreds.

Our honorary assistant secretary * has written this letter for your encouragement:

I would not have thought a year ago that I would be writing a progress report. Such a thought would have been outside the realms of possibility. At that time I was so deeply involved in the first major setback of my illness that to walk even a few paces from my front gate was enough to bring all the old terrifying symptoms. Failure piled upon failure.

At no time did I lose faith in Dr. Weekes's treatment, but I did lose belief I could make it work for me. However with the support of the journals, I managed somehow to carry on practicing but in a very feeble way. I was frequently in such deep despair I felt what little effort I was making was too much, especially as I seemed to be getting nowhere. The prospect of giving

* A small committee is responsible for distribution and financial management of the journals.

up altogether was very tempting, although this too filled me with a feeling of hopelessness. This was where it became important for me to remember to "let time pass," if you see what I mean.

After some months I began to win small victories and was able to look back from one week to the last and see I had progressed, although there were still dark days; but after more time, even these became fewer. One day I was actually able to say I felt better and more at ease.

At this stage progress seemed to speed up (the word "speed" is purely relative here), although it was still some time before bad days just didn't happen any more. Now I feel relaxed and free to move around. I will not pretend I still haven't a long way to go, but I can view the prospect with optimism rather than dread. How glad I am I did not give up! To fellow sufferers I would say: "Never give up. Keep practicing and letting time pass." I know some of you will think: "Oh yes, it is all right for her to talk, but I just couldn't do it." But I know you can because I have come up from just those depths of suffering and despair you are now in, and courage is not one of my strong points. Believe me, from personal experience I can say that if you keep faith with the teaching in these journals, you will eventually win through.

So:

- See the first days through.
- A mind refreshed is a mind unchained.
- You take your real home with you.
- Do not leave your mind behind in a house.
- Ride the first shock. Go slowly, and the difficult moment will pass.

JOURNAL 4: Floating, Physical Illness and Setback, Flash Experiences, Loneliness, Low Tranquilization

Although much in these journals has been about fear of leaving the safety of home, the advice given can be used to help with other fears and problems. For example, the person concerned about feeling unreal has probably learned by now to understand this and not be too impressed by it. A feeling of unreality is a natural result of too much introspection and self-analysis, which brings withdrawal from outside interests. *One should learn not to place too much importance on strange feelings in nervous illness. I stress this.* A nervously ill person can be impressed so easily by unusual emotional reactions of the moment because these can be made so intense and so flashing by sensitization. Flash experiences in nervous illness are discussed later.

Even obsession—as I have so often explained—is so often no more than loss of mental "resilience" through extreme fatigue; it need not be a sign of a deep-seated neurotic tendency asserting itself, as some of my patients had been told. Often the nature of the obsession does not upset as much as the habit itself. Many obsessions are surprisingly unimportant in themselves, although they bring such suffering. Cure lies in accepting the presence of the obsession for the time being and in not trying desperately to get rid of it. Acceptance relieves tension and so relieves the fatigue that keeps the obsession "engraved" on the tired mind. As one man put it, "It is as if the top, thinking part of my brain won't work, and the lower feeling part takes over." He really hit the nail on the head.

I repeat: Even those who believe their illness is much more complicated than agoraphobia can cure themselves by applying the advice given in these journals, which is based on those four principles—facing, accepting, floating, and letting time pass. *Of course, understanding must stand beside acceptance.* I know this sounds simpler than it is in practice, but I assure you once again that it will not fail if you persevere with it.

FLOATING

I have often been asked: "Just what do you mean by floating, Doctor?," so perhaps I should describe it more fully. Floating is the opposite of fighting. It means *to go with* the feelings, offering no tense resistance, just as, if floating on calm water, you would let your body go this way and that with the undulating waves. Let the moment of intense suffering float past you or through you. Do not arrest it or stay balked by it. Loosen toward it. Let your body go slack before it. Can you understand this? Some will think: "How can I float past a whipping lash of panic?" You can, by waiting without resistance until the lash spends itself and then by going on with the job at hand.

I speak here about letting the moment of suffering float past you, and again I sometimes speak of your floating through the moment. Floating can take many forms—you can imagine yourself floating forward through a moment of tense suffering, or you can imagine letting the suffering float through, and then away from, you. They amount to the same thing—it is the "letting go" implied by the words "float" and "floating" which matters. The important point is that floating is the opposite of fighting.

Although waiting without resistance may sound like doing nothing, it differs from apathetic doing nothing because when practicing floating, you are prepared to go forward and face and accept. When you do this, you are indeed doing a great deal. Apathy means no longer trying. One man wrote: "Dr. Weekes says, 'Accept and let time pass,' but I can't go on letting time pass. I've waited long enough doing nothing about it!" *I have never advised "doing nothing about it."* You will never recover by gazing at the ceiling.

A young girl described her experience with floating. It may help you. She said that on one occasion she was so tensed and agitated when trying to enter a bank that she suddenly stood stock still, locked in tension. She tried to push herself forward, but this made her feel more rooted to the pavement than ever. Then she remembered about "floating." She said, "I stretched my arms out a little and imagined I had wings and was floating through. It worked!"

"WHAT IS THE POINT OF TRYING AGAIN?"

I have guided you through the past months, trying to gauge your progress—or lack of it—and trying to plan each journal to coincide with the stage of your illness. If you are progressing at the same rate as my patients in Australia—the usual rate—you are probably ready for a talk on setback. Although some of you have made train journeys, driven your car alone, started doing your own shopping at last, you may now—because of physical illness, extra domestic tension, tension at work, or for no apparent reason—find yourselves in a setback that seems especially devastating after the early excitement of tasting a little freedom. You think, "If I can do all that and yet slip back so far, what is the point of trying again? Why go on struggling if it only leads to this?"

NERVOUS ILLNESS IS A VERY LONELY BUSINESS

Also, the family may begin to lose patience more than ever. The treatment sounds so simple to them. They may say, "Why can't you do what the doctor says? She says just what we have been saying all along! Take no notice of it! Forget it!" If only they could understand. A husband (or wife) who has spent years being patient may suddenly find himself so allergic to your illness that he can hardly bear to hear it mentioned; this can happen just when you need him so desperately to help you over these last disappointing hurdles. To you it seems so little to ask of him —that he stand by a while longer and not fail now when he is needed most. This may all add up to having recovery just within your grasp and then feeling it slip through your fingers for lack of extra help at a vital moment. Nervous illness can be a very lonely business.

Success comes to the one who goes on despite everything. You haven't a hope of winning the race unless you are in it. Be assured that once you decide to stay beside the triers, even after a severe setback you rarely have to retrace exactly the same painful steps when you begin to work at recovery again. The memory of past successes will come and strengthen your renewed effort. Also, *understanding now stands beside you.*

So do not keep comparing present poor performance with past success. Do not fall into the trap of thinking, "Last week I could do that easily. Now look at me! I'm as bad as ever!" Do not allow last week's success to magnify this week's failure. Simply take each setback as an occasion for further practice.

COPE WITH YOURSELF, NOT A SITUATION

After a particularly successful month one woman planned to make a trip she had previously found extremely difficult. It was driving alone down a long, lonely, narrow country road. She wanted to see how she would manage now with her newly found confidence. I explained that her anxious wish to test herself could make her apprehensive and that this, together with memory, could make that journey a disappointment. This is why I always stress learning how to cope with yourself and not how to cope with a particular situation. With repeated practice at coping with oneself until finally successful, you will find one situation means little more than another. When you review your past efforts, the efforts themselves have not varied so much, whatever the situation, have they? Your field of endeavor is really a narrow one after all—no wider than coping with the feelings within you, feelings that, as explained in my book and records, conform to a set pattern.

A specially difficult situation is no more than one that holds a greater number of difficult moments within yourself. These moments are not so very different from each other. They differ mostly in the *amount* of suffering and —what is so important—are not necessarily related to the importance of a situation. It is possible to have one's worst moment on what appears to be a very ordinary occasion. When panic sweeps, it sweeps, and when a sensitized person is going through a particularly bad spell, there may be very little variation in the intensity of the panic he feels. Try to remember this, and let it help you not to be unduly afraid of any special occasion or unduly impressed by a particularly severe wave of panic. This is why practicing right-reaction readiness, even at home, can help you cope with any situation by teaching you to cope with yourself.

PHYSICAL ILLNESS AND SETBACK

Many of the symptoms of physical ill health are the same as nervous symptoms—for example, palpitations, weakness, breathlessness, giddiness. The sufferer, after a bout of physical illness, has only to feel these symptoms mildly to be instantly reminded of all his other nervous symptoms. Memory works like a chain reaction. With fear and disappointment added, he may find himself in a setback; and this, together with the debility brought by the physical illness (possibly influenza), may make recovery seem remote.

YOU DO NOT HEAL YOURSELF

If allowed, time and nature will heal you. Remember that you do not have to heal yourself. Nature is ready to do it if you step out of her way and do not present her with those unnecessary obstacles despair and disappointment. You remember to take your tranquilizers (how some of you remember!); why not take a dose of nature three times a day? Say to yourself after each meal, "Over to nature. I'll try not to hinder her by defeatist thinking."

So:

- Go with the feelings.
- Wait without resistance. Let your body slacken.
- You will never recover by gazing at the ceiling.
- Nervous illness can be a lonely business. You may not feel so lonely when you remember the many others tramping the same way, however.
- Understanding now stands beside you.
- Learn to cope with yourself, not with a particular place.
- A special occasion is no more than another occasion for you to practice *coping with yourself*.

FLASH EXPERIENCES

In my L.P. recordings I said that if asked to pinpoint the most disturbing aspect of setback, I would say it is the return of panic when the sufferer thought he was cured. I would now like to add to this the recurrence of strange feelings that come occasionally, usually when least expected.

By strange feelings I mean feelings that are difficult to describe—for example, a sudden feeling of dissolution, of disintegration, of impending disaster or death; sudden flashes of agitation; depression; apprehension; unreality; depersonalization. These feelings come at any time, perhaps even during an animated conversation when the sufferer may be at his best and may even have forgotten his illness for the time being. Their effect can be so shocking he may suddenly be arrested in the middle of a sentence, a laugh. He may then think despairingly that he is able to go only so far toward recovery and will never completely recover.

The sufferer should learn to see these strange moments as no more than *flash experiences* of no real significance. He must wait quietly for them to pass. *They will always pass,* and when not allowed to balk him, will become no more significant than an occasional unhappy memory such as we all have from time to time. Most people have collected a few strange thoughts over the years, which recur from habit and must be lived with. Life gives so much time to collect bizarre thoughts and feelings. When treated as unimportant, they are eventually hardly noticed; at least, they cause little disturbance.

It is a mistake to look for reasons for these flash experiences. They should not be tracked down, analyzed, and so unnecessarily accentuated. They are not worth it. Some, at least, occur to most sufferers during recovery and are a result of the suffering they have been through; they mean no more than that. Flash experiences have no bearing on the future, so do not let them spoil a moment you may be enjoying. Be prepared for the moment of shock and despair that they bring, and pass through it without letting it distract you too much.

RECOVER   CANNOT   BE   HURRIED

The honorary assistant secretary's letter in Journal 3 has encouraged some of you to take great strides; however, I always keep in mind those who still find the way difficult and who think progress, if any, is too slow. Try not to be upset by slow progress, and above all do not be discouraged by your age. However old you are, you could not, in your present state, be spending your time a better way than by working toward recovery. So do not begrudge the time you give. Go quietly, at your own pace. No one can hasten recovery, not even for the sake of those they love most. Hurry brings more tension. One can, of course, slow up recovery by not going forward enough often enough. When I speak of hastening recovery, I mean feverishly trying to force the pace.

Never let setback put you out of the race. Toe the line again, and practice the way I teach you. The teaching will not fail. Examine any failure, and you will see that at a particular moment you did not have the courage to go forward. *You withdrew at the peak of suffering* and did not see it through. You shrank once more into yourself. No setback, however severe, can keep you from recovery if you are still willing to go on. *Recovery always lies ahead in the doing.*

LONELINESS

I wish to speak to those living alone, and this also means housewives who are alone all day, especially those whose husbands will not discuss their illness with them—indeed, in a few instances, will not discuss much with them. A habit of fear is harder to lose in loneliness because one's talking is mainly to oneself, and nervously ill people are especially poorly equipped to take their own advice. They have let themselves down too often in the past to be impressed by their own encouragement. Also, it is only too easy to repeat an upsetting habit when alone; there is so little diversion to discourage habit.

You are not quite as alone as you have been in the past, however. As I mentioned earlier, understanding now stands beside you. Also, the knowledge that you are one of many people following the advice in these journals may bring a sense of fellowship.

By degrees this understanding helps relax your attitude, even toward yourself—even toward loneliness—and as you become less interested in your own suffering, naturally you become more interested in outside events. In the long run the best cure for loneliness is occupation among people, and each must find this in his or her own way. It is frustrating for all concerned that finding congenial work in good company should be as difficult as it is.

If you are trained for work but have not had the courage to leave home to find it, pluck up that courage now and make the effort. *Do not be put off if at first you fail at the job.* You may have to go through many hours of misery before you accustom yourself to working again. Be willing to try; as I said before, you have no hope of winning the race unless you are in it. Fail as often as necessary, but no failure is as great as the failure to make the effort.

I wish each of you had some interest to help you face the day. Try to find an interest. If you should think of taking a job, do not be put off by any traveling involved; surely for a while someone would take you? If you have the courage to take the plunge and find work, don't be discouraged by any experience you may have during those first weeks. Those early weeks could not possibly be easy, anxious as you are. Go with the tide, "tread water," until the worst is over. If you do this, the difficulties will iron out, and you will find yourself gradually feeling secure in a routine that becomes familiar at last.

While at work or at home, if you are practicing my teaching, there may be times when you feel quite like your old self, only to find a little later that the moment has slipped away to leave you disappointed, weary. Wait. The happy experience will come again some other time. *Do not try to force it or hasten its return.* If you do, you will only frighten it further away.

So:

- Never let setback put you out of the race.
- Try not to withdraw at the peak of suffering. This is the most important moment.
- Go with the tide, tread water, until the worst is over.

ACHIEVEMENT MUST BECOME ROUTINE

Recovery has its moments of spectacular achievement, but for any achievement to be established as recovery it must become routine. When this happens, it may fail to impress you, and you may think you have made little progress. If you compare what you can do today with what you did a year ago, however, you will surely find you have made progress. There may be nothing spectacular or even encouraging about consolidating earlier successes, but *so much depends on consolidation.* Do not be afraid to give time to this, even if it means repeating often something you know you can now do well. Every little bit adds up and makes a firmer springboard to help you toward greater achievement.

One woman said recently: "What is the use of trying to go there? I know I can do it now." Knowing you "can do it" is not enough. If you rest too much on past achievement, you may find to your surprise that the next time you have to "do it," you will have to break ground all over again. Repeated doing is always the answer.

The following letter came from the woman mentioned

in an earlier journal who could not "make" the town center:

> Those who are still bogged down by the thought "I can't do it!" may be interested to know how I managed to break through a little by deciding to really try to accept all that might come my way.
>
> I have been trying Dr. Weekes's method since last September, starting by walking down the street a few yards. I did this daily unless I felt extremely bad—and gradually extended the distance. After a while the short walks became easier and easier. However, instead of feeling elated, I felt dissatisfied. I was not satisfied with a small taste of freedom. I wanted complete freedom.
>
> My problem really started now, as I have not been able to bear my husband out of my sight for years. I went daily to his shop with him. This might sound wonderful to some lonely sufferers, but I assure you the dependency was crippling. I decided there was only one way to break it. I had to get a job. Of course, the mere thought of this brought back every symptom, but I had to choose between two evils. So I found work. I went for the interview, bearing the feelings as best as I was able, and started my part-time job.
>
> The first few days were terrible. I was separated from my husband; I had to take responsibility and was sometimes left in charge of the office, so that I couldn't walk out if I wanted to. I told no one of my illness. When I felt bad, I found taking a deep breath and letting it out slowly helped. I told myself it would all pass. And it did. My confidence grew until I could start off for work feeling only uncomfortable but knowing I could cope.
>
> After nine weeks I had to leave the office, as there was

not enough work for two. I kept thinking they had found me inadequate and that I was no like other people. Along came setback. My self-confidence sank so low the thought of another job filled me with horror. I was also depressed by the waste of the effort I had so dearly made.

I had discovered by working like other people most of the physical symptoms had left me, but depression and exhaustion remained. Yet I felt it was better to be depressed and exhausted when doing than to have all the other symptoms that came when I was not doing. Now locked at home once more, it was not long before I was flooded with the old feelings. Eventually, I realized I had to get another job. This time I went for the interview not caring whether I got it or not. This must have been a sort of acceptance; because I can honestly say I was not nervous, and they took me on.

I started working, and to my amazement, I did not feel too bad. My previous efforts were paying dividends. I have now been employed for three weeks. I still feel very tired, even slightly depressed, but I have a feeling this will pass. Through taking a *big* step I find I can do smaller things more easily. To act normal makes me feel normal. I have found the thought of doing is far worse than the actual doing. I am even at the stage where I almost welcome nervous feelings so I can accept and watch them pass. This is a step toward coping with myself. Good luck to you all. Please try. It pays dividends.

One man wrote: "Since receiving your help, I have started work in a fairly responsible job, but I cannot see myself completely cured. I frighten myself too much." At this stage this man should be reconciled to frightening himself for the time being. As I have said again and again, how can anyone expect to forget quickly fears that have upset him for so long? How could he quickly lose a habit of frightening himself while fear strikes at the slightest thought?

If he accepts frightening himself *as a habit to be expected at the moment* and if he continues working with this habit and does not immediately think that because of it, he will not recover, his very acceptance will gradually desensitize him, and in time he will be able to think about being frightened without necessarily immediately feeling afraid. This does not mean that if he does this, he will never feel severe panic again. Of course he may. If, however, he applies the same principle each time and passes through the panic willingly, it will finally lose its power to dominate him—as it does now. *This takes time.*

He is especially vulnerable at the moment in his new, and more responsible, job. He wants so much to hold it that he is probably constantly anxious about the way he feels. What more fertile soil could fear find? He should understand this also and not expect too much from himself for the time being.

SECOND FEAR NEVER COMES UNBIDDEN

Some of you may think that sometimes you do not frighten yourselves but that panic comes unbidden and that this is why recovery may seem so difficult for you. It is true that panic, as *first* fear, may seem to flash unbidden on occasions, but *second* fear (the fear you add yourself to *first* fear) never comes unbidden.

The above letter from the man was obviously written in *second* fear. This is why I teach seeing panic through, learning to function with panic there, and not waiting anxiously to be free of it. Cure does not necessarily lie in being rid of panic. Cure lies in being willing to cope with panic when it comes and in being willing to let it take its own time to go because—believe me—it will take its own time. You can only hasten its going by not withdrawing from it.

SCUTTLING BACK TO YOUR SAFETY ZONE

Real cure begins when panic does not send you scuttling back to your safety zone. The first time you discover panic no longer matters may seem so strange that you could feel frightened by the significance of your new discovery, and then, of course, panic can suddenly matter again. It seemed too good to be true. It takes time for sensitized reaction to the thought of panic no longer to bring panic. Time, time, is still the answer, and willingness to pass through panic again and again if necessary. Always remember "willingness" (free reaction) is the key.

LOW TRANQUILIZATION

A woman wrote, "I am disturbed by the anxious feeling that comes when tranquilization is low." The anxious feeling that comes when tranquilization is low is really two feelings. One is the restlessness that sometimes accompanies the diminishing effect of the tranquilizer, and the other is the anxiety the sufferer feels when he realizes the effect of his tablet is due to come to an end. He knows when to expect this and waits anxiously for the time. As soon as he swallows another pill he feels better, even before it has had time to dissolve in his stomach.

Anxiety about low tranquilization may have as great an effect on one's body as low tranquilization itself. Here again, nature would gradually compensate for the effect of low tranquilization if the sufferer would give it a chance. *Remember nature is always trying to adjust your body back to normal.* That is her constant task. The agitation that may come with low tranquilization must lessen if we hand the job over to nature and wait with acceptance.

Agitation, although so disturbing, does no harm. It will always pass if you do not become agitated because you are agitated. Beware of *second* fear to the best of your ability. One woman, whose doctor withdrew her tranquilization, wrote, "I did have withdrawal symptoms in the beginning, which were unpleasant but only to be expected after four years of being on tablets. Because my body is no longer used to being constantly tranquilized, I now find half a tablet taken occasionally calms immediately." Nature does do her work if you will let her.

I do not wish to minimize the effects of withdrawal of tranquilizers and am not asking you to stop your tablets. Some of you need them for the time being. In my opinion, if you take tranquilizers, the dosage should not be decreased until you have accustomed yourself to moving more easily. As you recover, you will find from time to time you forget to take them. What a good sign this is!

Of course, some of you may be taking so many tablets during the day or night that the constant tiredness and possible depression you are perhaps feeling could be caused by this medication and not by "nerves," as you now believe. Here it is essential to check with your doctor.

JOURNAL 5: Special Encouragement, Home from Vacation

SPECIAL ENCOURAGEMENT

In past journals I have written mostly for those who have not been particularly successful. Now I draw attention to you who have done well because recently some depressing opinions have been expressed publicly about curing fears and phobias, and I want to emphasize once more, as I did in the previous journal, that fears and phobias—and this includes agoraphobia—are indeed curable. Success must always depend on the treatment given as well as on the patient, and the essence of treatment is to teach the sufferer to go where he meets his fears, not only understanding them but also knowing how to cope with fear itself.

AGORAPHOBIA IS DIFFERENT

Coping with specific fears, such as fear of animals, darkness, thunderstorms, is different from coping with fear of traveling alone away from home. One can be taught to gradually look at and think of spiders, for instance, without fear because this fear is of something *apart from oneself*. Agoraphobia is different. It is the fear of fear *within oneself*. If you are afraid of spiders, you fear the look, the feel, the bite, even the thought, of the spider. If agoraphobic, you aren't afraid of the school hall, the restaurant, the train, the subway, in the same way. You are not afraid of the actual places; you are afraid of the feeling of panic and the other sensations you have in these places. You are afraid of what is actually happening within yourself, afraid you will be unable to cope with it and of what this might lead to—quite a different matter. I emphasize this point. So if agoraphobia is given the same treatment as any other phobia, disappointing results are understandable. Agoraphobia requires a treatment of its own.

COURAGE WAS NOT THEIR STRONG POINT

According to reports, our honorary assistant secretary's letter seems to have helped many of you because she said bravery was not one of her strong points. Many clung to this. They thought that if she could do it, then perhaps they too, who felt in their hearts bravery was not their strong point either, might have a chance.

To go out and face dreaded experiences does need

courage. There is no question of this, but I am trying to show you that if you do it with the right attitude—with acceptance through understanding—by the laws of physiology themselves, you dull the edge of terror, if not immediately, at least gradually (although it can happen immediately). Actually, if you could realize it, you need less courage to face what comes when you truly accept than when you go forward grimly under the tension of clenched determination.

The method I teach is a potent weapon in your defense because it is nature's way. Some of the reports in this journal show how readers who have not traveled for years can now travel freely at home and abroad by using this method.

Some nervously ill people are said to be of "poor potential" and are accepted as "chronics." It can certainly be disheartening for a doctor to interview for the first time a patient accompanied by a thick pile of case-history sheets, including discouraging reports from other clinics; however, the fact that the patient is actually sitting in the chair beside the doctor means he has a little hope left, and if the doctor can also find hope, good work can still be done. I have sometimes found that at the moment when I was tempted to think a certain man or woman would never make the grade he or she showed the first glimmer of understanding and made the first step forward. It is essential that both patient and doctor stay hopeful. Hope is not merely a feeling. *It is also action—the first positive step toward recovery.*

WHILE YOU WANT TO RECOVER, YOU CAN

The wish to recover is the real potential. To put it another way: While you wish to recover, you can. So however badly you may think you have failed so far, if you still want to be cured, *you have the potential.* No matter what the family thinks, no matter what anyone might think, *you've got it. You have it there.* Of course, you recover more quickly if someone is helping you. And yet many of you are working from my book, journals, and records alone. I wish I could give you personal help, but this is impossible. Even if there is no one to help you, you can still manage by yourselves.

DON'T WAIT TOO LONG FOR CONFIDENCE TO RETURN

Some will say, "I know what Doctor Weekes means, but I just couldn't do it." That is not good enough. There is no one who cannot do it. You can do it. Unfortunately, you have let failure disconcert and discourage you so much that you now wait for confidence to come back of its own accord. Do not wait too long for confidence to return. It is regained only when you begin to do the things you think you cannot do. Even if the beginning is so small that you can hardly recognize it as a beginning, it is still action, and *confidence is built on action.* You can sit at home and imagine yourself doing this or that, as I suggested in my discussion of right-reaction readiness, but all the imagining in the world will not bring confidence *unless you follow imagination with action.*

It is not only the doing but also the knowledge that you know how you have done it which is important. The aim of some treatments today is to condition patients to act—especially travel—suppressing fear. When conditioned in this way, though, are these patients acting with confidence? Suddenly a sight, sound, smell—anything that reminds them of their fears—may start them panicking again. Do they know how to cope with panic? I doubt it.

This is why I teach you the hard way—by *passing through panic to peace*—and it is because it is the hard way that some of you think you have failed so far. Don't blame yourself at this stage if you think you are among the failures. I am asking a lot from you, but the final reward is worth the effort. In the end you will have the confidence to cope with fear, but this takes time, so take fresh heart.

Some of your reports were especially pleasing. You admitted you still expected further setbacks but were learning how to cope with them. People who have been led forward too gently either by having their emotions constantly calmed by drugs or merely by suggestion could find themselves very bewildered in a setback.

I want to qualify the statement "by drugs." From reports, some of you seem to think I am not in favor of tranquilization. This is not true. I said in the beginning that if you were severely sensitized, you might need enough tranquilization to take the edge off your too-sensitized reactions, and here, of course, your doctor could help you.

HE NEED NOT GO WITHOUT SOME TRANQUILIZATION

In my practice I give tranquilizers as I judge necessary and reduce dosage gradually. One of the journal subscribers had changed his job for a more responsible one and said that although he was doing well, he felt he needed the help of some sedation during the day. He added that he thought I would be disappointed about this. Not so. I do not expect him at this stage to do without such help. He may need help until he grows more used to the work. I know that panic can cut through tranquilization enough to give him opportunity to practice coping with it. There is no point in enduring the added stress of a new job without some temporary help. I am for moderation in all things, even in one's attitude to tranquilizers. I make no hard and fast rule. In this matter you must be guided by your doctor.

"I DON'T KNOW HOW I GOT BETTER!"

A person who has recovered from nervous illness simply by time bringing him out of it—with no special treatment —usually says, "I don't know how it happened. I just seemed to get better." I am always a little anxious for such people because should circumstances sensitize them once more and should they then become frightened, they can only hope they will come out of their fears as they did before—blindly. They often live in the shadow of apprehension. If you think my teaching is difficult, be cheered by the knowledge that this very difficulty, once coped with, will be your strength in the years to come.

TO FIND SOMEONE WHO UNDERSTANDS THE TERROR

In one report a woman wrote:

I have been ill on and off since 1944, so I do not expect to recover in an instant. Looking back on last year, even I can see how much better I am. I can now take the car to go shopping alone. You cannot imagine how wonderful it has been to find someone who understands the terror and real hell one goes through. I didn't think it possible, and the fact that you know one's feelings so well has done as much to help me as anything. It is especially hard to make people realize how awful one feels when one is plump and healthy looking—and I've not lost weight; in fact, I've put it on, and apart from turning a ghastly color sometimes, I look fit to those who don't know me well.

It is perhaps the feeling of utter exhaustion which I still find most trying, and I so often feel that if I could only get my strength back, I could cope so much better with the business of recovery. I'm still frightened (petrified would be more correct) of going any distance from home—that is to New York or on vacation. However, I feel by next year I shall be able to do these things, even if a little uncomfortably. I shall have a go. I still have giddiness, and this is what started me off on the road to nerves. However, I am now able to cope with giddiness and loss of balance by floating and letting time pass. Now and again I get flashes of confidence which are especially super.

Nervous exhaustion follows so much emotional suffering. It is sometimes the last symptom to go. It does pass.
So:

- Acceptance with understanding dulls the edge of terror.
- *In the final count,* it takes less effort, even less courage, to go forward with true acceptance than to go forward fighting grimly.
- Hope is action, not merely a feeling.
- While you want to recover, you can.
- There is no one who cannot do it. You can do it.
- Confidence comes only when you begin to do the things you think you cannot do.
- Pass through panic to peace.

SITTING WITH HER COAT ON

Another woman wrote:

I can manage a short walk on my own and find that if I can do it on the spur of the moment, I am much better. It's the sitting, waiting with my coat on, and trying to make up my mind that builds up the tension. As the evenings draw in, I'm going to try to go further afield in the dark. My biggest problem doing the short walks is the fear that people are looking at me, especially if I have to turn round quickly and come home. I convince myself that outwardly I look no different from anyone else, but the feelings still persist.

I am able to get over the panic. Now, I just sit and wait for it to pass. Recently a kind neighbor called and asked me to go shopping with her. Although I've been going out only with my husband, I thought, "Here goes!"

and I went and thoroughly enjoyed myself. I could not have done that six months ago. These may seem trivial things, but as you can imagine, they mean a great deal to me.

Let me look at that letter and see how much I can help that woman. Her trouble, of course, is mainly anticipation. When she anticipates, she should say to herself, "If waiting is so bad and yet I manage it, surely I can manage going out?"

It is not only the nervous person who feels some apprehension when going on a trip. If one has been very happy staying with friends or even has to leave home to go on vacation, the day of departure, even the day before departure, may bring a slight feeling of unpleasant apprehension. I call these the departure blues. One who has had the habit of staying home for a long time would naturally feel this way to a strong degree if faced with moving far from home and to some extent when only contemplating moving a short distance away. Going anywhere out of the house becomes a real uprooting, and this is not all nervous illness.

WAITING IS A MOST TRYING EXPERIENCE

So if you have the chance of going out on the spur of the moment, do so. If you must wait before leaving, understand that waiting is one of the most trying experiences and that it may continue to agitate and upset you for some time to come. Be cheered by the thought that if you manage the waiting—as I have taught you—you will have gone a long way toward managing the rest. You haven't gone out alone enough yet, you haven't succeeded enough yet, to be able to go out without some tense anticipation. *Time, more time, more doing:* This is the answer. Anticipation is one of the last difficulties to go, and doing things well one day and badly the next doesn't help anticipation one little bit!

Naturally, the woman who wrote the letter has the feeling people will watch her when she turns back. If any of us, on setting off from home, remember something we have forgotten to bring with us—or a faucet left running—and turn suddenly round and walk in the opposite direction, we feel rather foolish. So much of what you think is illness is natural reaction under the circumstances. You turn such strong searchlights on your every action and every thought that you set a standard of behavior for yourself the non-nervous person does not bother even to think about. So do not be upset if you "feel funny" and think people notice. Seeing someone turn suddenly is not important to the passerby. Try to make it unimportant to yourself. Turn again, but this time in the right direction.

A man wrote on behalf of his wife, "I read your book in bed to my wife at night. Within two months a remarkable change has come over her. Her attitude has altered. However, she is not completely free because she finds meeting people socially still very difficult."

Mixing with other people is difficult for the nervously ill person, not necessarily because they are shy by nature but because they are usually, due to their illness, trying to do two different things at the same time. First they try to listen to what the other person is saying so that they can give some kind of sensible answer, and yet at the same time they are listening intently to their own thoughts about how terrible it is to have so little confidence, to feel so confused, and to be in such an upsetting situation.

This dual role makes them feel like two people—one struggling to carry on a conversation while the other stands by listening, undermining. It would be a difficult task for anyone and a harrowing experience for the nervously ill person, who needs so little to agitate and confuse him. Is it any wonder such a person avoids meeting people? It is essential, however, for the woman mentioned in this letter (and for all like her) to understand that this strange experience must be lived through with acceptance many times before she will be more interested in the other person's conversation than in her own feelings and thoughts —in other words, until she can be natural.

GO PREPARED TO FEEL STRANGE

I hope this explanation gives some of you the courage to go out and get the practice you need. Go prepared to feel strange, to not follow much of the conversation, to feel awkward, even in another world, sometimes perhaps to make strange answers, but at the same time to know that while you feel this way, so do many others, and that to go through this experience is an expected part of recovery. How strange recovery can be and yet not so strange when one realizes every phase is shared by someone else.

There is nothing odd about recovery, nothing unique about it, nothing really strange about it, except to you who experience it. What a well-trodden path it really is. There is no other way of getting used to meeting people than first to go through the difficult process of meeting them.

REPETITION CAN IMPRESS THE PATTERN OF YOUR ILLNESS

So much in nervous illness is weariness of doing the same thing, meeting the same people, repeating the same routine. Repetition can so easily impress upon you the pattern of your illness. One repeats the same performance almost as if under compulsion. Even the progress you have made seems part of the old pattern, when repeated often enough. Going out, meeting new people, widens your horizon and gives you something new to talk about and, what is more important, something new to think about. This refreshes; the old tracks of suffering are given some respite, so that when one returns to them, they do not sear quite so severely.

Remember that failure is part of recovery. I have not seen a patient recover without first failing somewhere, somehow. So however you fail, you are still in the mainstream with many others. Recovery is still there, waiting for you.

There are many letters I would have liked to include here to cheer you. Here is one cheerful note: "We have had a wonderful vacation this year, and I have just moved. I can now go about freely and have no tranquilization. If I am a little apprehensive about a journey, I carry the journal or your book in my bag. If a spasm comes, I can carry on working and know it is not important and will pass." Bravo.

Another woman wrote, "More often than not I can float through the frightening symptoms. It is easier now to toss them over my shoulder. The biggest problem, which has lasted many years, is tension, and this makes muscles ache in a different place each day. Despite this, the difference and improvement is amazing. I'm sure I'll win through one day." I'm sure she will too.

A happy mother wrote, "Today, October 1, will go down in history for me. After twelve weeks of learning to drive, I took the car out of the garage myself this morning and picked up my young son from school for the first time. I was really jittery and said to myself, "Come on! You've got so far; don't give in!" And taking my courage in both hands, I did it. I had never taken drugs, so I have to rely on my own strength and the help in these articles. It's like conquering Everest, but I know now it can be done."

So:

- Departure blues are natural. Reluctance to move far from home is not all nervous illness.

- When you have managed waiting, you have gone a long way toward managing the rest.
- Tense anticipation is one of the last experiences to go.
- So much nervous illness is no more than natural reaction under the circumstances—but very much exaggerated.

HOME FROM VACATION

After vacationing successfully away from home, you may dread returning to your restricted orbit. What you think of as your orbit is not so much barriers in locality beyond which you will not travel as barriers in thought—mental blocks—beyond which you shrink from thinking. You are restricted by a habit of thought to the tracks you have followed for so long. So when you return home, it is so easy to fall into the old way of restricting movement within the familiar orbit. This is understandable because at home so much reminds you of the old pattern, thus disarming you and weakening your resolve to extend your orbit.

Away from home you moved in new tracks, saw new sights and different people, heard new sounds. These made new images in your mind. Playing golf on a new course, swimming, walking, meant a whole set of new pictures. You felt different because you *were* different. *You were emerging from the grayness of repetition.*

As the day of leaving for home approaches, some of the old agitation could easily return. This is understandable. Don't immediately lose heart and think your vacation has done you no good, that you will never come out of your illness. It isn't easy to give up a new-found sense of freedom. It could be the first time you have tasted freedom after years of feeling caged, and it is not easy to stand by and watch it slip away.

You are also disappointed because you sense that if this

vacation could have lasted even a little longer, you could have consolidated the progress you made. As well as this, it isn't easy, having tasted freedom, to return to the place where the old restricted pattern of movement must be faced. It is almost as if the cage doors are waiting to shut behind you.

Take heart. After you pass through the first shock of being home, some of the newly found confidence will return. If the old suffering comes back when you reach home (and you may go looking for it before you even begin unpacking), do not immediately think, "What's the use?" and doubt you will recover. Most sufferers doubt. Recovery is such a new experience that you will surely misunderstand it, misinterpret it, because habit and memory are waiting to discourage you at every opportunity.

INTO THE WHIRLPOOL

However deep into the whirlpool of suffering you may go when you return, try to remember this grueling experience will end, though for the moment you may seem to lose contact with everything that means recovery. However deep, however tragic, the moment of setback may seem, try to glimpse that you are going through a temporary experience *that is still part of recovery.*

Have the courage to think, "Even if I have to go through the ultimate in suffering all over again, let it come!" Have you ever really faced the ultimate? The fear that can hold you back from doing so is the fear that can keep you straddling two worlds—the world of nervous illness and the world of recovery. So return with understanding and willingness to face whatever memories the old familiar scenes may bring, and know that memory and its fears are also part of recovery.

Try to remember:

- You are restricted by a habit of thought.

- However deep into the whirlpool you may go, the experience will pass.
- Invite the ultimate. When you do, the moment will melt.
- Setback and its fears are still part of recovery.

JOURNAL 6: Depression (Depletion), Change of Life, The Small Coffee Shop

DEPRESSION (DEPLETION)

Many of you have asked me to talk about depression. Although you may not realize it, you really want me to talk about "depletion" because the depression that comes to a person suffering with a nervous disturbance is so often based on physical depletion following so much anxious suffering for so long. Depletion can also depend on the depth of suffering, not necessarily on the length of time one has suffered. Vital resources are drained. There may still be a desire to do things and yet a feeling of inability to get started doing them, or there may be no desire to do anything. Sometimes desire may be fleeting—here one minute, gone the next—and all this makes ordinary living seem unendurable.

"HE COULD GET BETTER IF HE REALLY WANTED TO!"

It has been said that many nervously ill people could get well if they really wanted to. Do not let this statement worry you. I assure you that although it may be true for a few, the vast majority want to recover; however, when a person is depleted, recovery may seem so beyond his reach that it may *appear* he does not wish to make the effort. Even making an appointment a few days or weeks ahead may seem too much. To accept an invitation for lunch a week from Wednesday is more like a threat than a promise of enjoyment. The desire to go comes only in flashes —if it comes at all—and when the week arrives after days of dreaded anticipation bringing more tension and hence more depletion, it can hardly be counted on to give even one flash of positive desire to go. So on Tuesday night another ingenious excuse will be offered to cancel the appointment. What remorse, what bewilderment, what desperation of ever leading an ordinary life again, follow. Had the friend said, "Come today," the sufferer would have stood a chance of mustering courage and going, even if with inner turmoil. To plan ahead demands so much from a depleted person.

Packing a suitcase to go away is one of the most difficult tasks. It hardly matters how the case is packed or how the lid is closed. If someone else will pack it—even one of the children—so much the better. The packing may be started days before departure, so arduous is the task. How odd it all seems, how unendurable, how difficult to explain; and what guilt it brings, what misunderstanding from some relatives and friends.

"COME ON, MOTHER, COME AND SEE AUNTIE JESS!"

Depletion is one of the most discouraging experiences in nervous illness. It is difficult to understand, difficult to cope with, and it calls for a lot of sympathy for those who feel this way. Unfortunately, it may have such an effect on the family that the joy of living can be dampened for them also, with the result that they need sympathy themselves and may become incapable of giving it to the ill relative. Despairing families say, "Doctor, what are we to say? Everything we do or say seems to be wrong." A husband may say, "My wife is beginning to build up such hate toward me. I can't understand it. She used to be so loving. Now she can be quite nasty, and this is spoiling our relationship. What am I to do about this?"

This cycle can be stopped. Rarely has the family been coping the right way. How could they be expected to? They are not doctors. They are likely to say, "Come on, Mom! Come and see Auntie Jess!" or, "Come and have a game of cards with the Johnsons. It'll do you good!" Mother perhaps makes the effort but often returns only temporarily helped or more tired and dispirited than before she went. This is disappointing for the family but especially disappointing for the mother. Unfortunately, curing nervous depletion may take some months, and trying to push or pull the mother or father toward cure rarely helps.

The sufferer often calls depletion exhaustion, and it is close to exhaustion. I say "close to" because however exhausted we may think ourselves (from whatever nervous cause), we are never quite exhausted. There will always be enough strength left to run downstairs if a fire starts upstairs. Nevertheless, the depleted person often thinks himself completely exhausted. If you suffer like this and can think of your body as temporarily depleted, rather than depressed, and can understand that in time it can heal itself by recharging its emotional battery, hope comes into the picture.

THE "HORSE'S HOOF" ON THE CHEST

Look at the people around you. Most of them have no more in their lives to help them enjoy life than you would have if you were well. Why then is it so difficult for you to enjoy yourself? It is difficult because your usual vital responses are weak. There is either a "vacuum" where feeling should be, or there may be a feeling of heavy, pressing depression (the "horse's hoof") on chest or abdomen which may become so distressing that the cycle of depression goes on and on, bringing more exhaustion, more depletion, and so more depression. There is nothing so depressing as depression.

Depletion can work in many strange ways. Anything

that usually is only slightly off-putting may seem exceptionally so; a depleted person may tremble before the slightest tense experience. Also, what previously had normally seemed no more than odd—for example, something as simple as a carved wooden figure—may appear disturbingly grotesque to a depleted person. While reactions to the unimportant, such as the wooden carving, can be exaggerated, one's reactions to more important situations seem weak or even absent.

When you understand depression as part of depletion (extreme fatigue), accept it as a physical state, and are prepared to wait patiently (very difficult!) for your emotional battery to recharge itself, a time comes when you can talk to yourself encouragingly and *feel* the encouragement mean something at last. You can almost feel yourself lifting yourself up onto a higher level. You feel a little steadier, even though some of the sinking, exhausting feeling may still be present. For your own encouragement to mean something is indeed a step forward. In the depths of depression one feels one gets more help from others than from oneself, especially if they understand and do encourage. This is why one so often longs desperately for kind, helpful words from family or friends. Encouraging words seem as solid and supporting as a stout staff when said at the right time.

AS THE LIGHTS GO ON, SPIRITS USUALLY LIFT

One of the perplexing aspects of depletion is its return from time to time when one thought one had completely recovered. For example, the old bogey may raise his head at only a slight disappointment, a mildly melancholic atmosphere, slight tension, and so on. One is reminded that reserves are still inadequate to cushion these experiences. Also, any one of us has moments when life seems less inviting than at others. Dusk is an ebb for many, especially if the family that once returned at this time has now scattered. As the lights go on and the evening settles, however, spirits usually lift. So do not allow dusk to unduly depress you. Think of the thousands of others who share these moments with you, and maybe you will feel less lonely.

Some people are in such a state of depletion that they need complete rest, and this is when I recommend sedation —not heavy, but enough to keep the sufferer contented to do little for a week or two. The stage of severe agitated depletion does not last long if adequately treated and willingly accepted, especially if it is passed in surroundings that give some diversion and encouragement. Unfortunately, such surroundings are not always easy to find, despite the family's endeavors.

"I'D LIKE TO SEE MYSELF PUTTER ABOUT WITH ALL THIS WORK TO DO!"

If adequately treated, the sufferer should be able to putter about by the end of a month. Those forced to continue at work may think, "I'd like to see myself putter about, with all this work to do!" I am now talking about only a few extremely fatigued people, however. The majority of letters coming from those of you complaining of depression and exhaustion show most of you can, and still do, manage to cope with the day's work. If you are like this, it helps to remember that this is a physical condition and that it has arisen partly through exhausting a flat battery. If you do not want to make the effort to play cards with the Johnsons, do not make it, and do not feel guilty because you have not. You must, though, *at the same time*, have an attitude of moving *toward recovery*. When I advise not making a certain effort, I do not mean you should make *no* effort. Use common sense. Waiting as optimistically as possible, without whipping yourself along, is more help than continuously trying to force a weary body. I use the word "continuously" because unless you sometimes make an effort, you quickly lose confidence in being able to do so. I know it is not easy for a nervously ill person to decide what is the sensible thing to do, so let me say that whatever course you take, *if you take it willingly* and *go with it,* you will be on the right track.

NATURE'S GIFT

The vitality that brings interest to even the small happenings of every day is our legacy as human beings. It is there for each of us. Do not be misled by your temporarily depleted vitality into thinking ordinary living is not interesting. When you are revitalized, even going to see if the plumber has done what we asked of him can be interesting and not just another chore. It is because you are as you are that ordinary living may seem humdrum, depressing. Remember this and be prepared to take each day as it comes (especially the mornings). Say to yourself: "My store of vitality is low, because my body has been whipped by anxiety. I have overdrawn on my emotional reserve; even so, my body will heal itself again if I will allow it. This is nature's gift."

It is not easy to say this and mean it when one's mood changes so quickly. Hope, despair, hope, despair: Will they ever level out into ordinary living? They will. As one recovers, however, it is sometimes difficult to know how much "not wanting to do" is a lazy habit and how much of it is genuinely due to remaining depletion. Extreme depletion brings such definite symptoms that it is only too readily felt and recognized as a physical state. As depletion eases and depression lifts, however, one does the obviously interesting things easily enough but still has the feeling of not enough interest to do the unpleasant things. There are many chores that most of us put off as long as we can—writing letters, mending, certain shopping, certain telephone calls, paying bills, and so on. Acute reluctance here is no more than normal reluctance exaggerated. Everything cannot suddenly be interesting. Everything is not interesting. So coming out of depletion and coping with the usually uninspiring jobs are always difficult but must be done to reach a level where ordinary living becomes worthwhile.

TRUST IN THE MIRACLE RESTORED VITALITY WILL BRING

Try not to let the depression of depletion overwhelm you. Trust in the miracle restored vitality will bring. If, for instance, while you wait for recovery, you find you can read only a little, that your concentration wanders, then read only a little. If you find it difficult to talk to people, hard to be interested in what they say, do not be upset by this. This too will pass, and you are not always to blame. Some conversations can be very dull. Think in terms of depletion, not depression. This helps because you can understand how a body can replenish itself, whereas it may be difficult to understand the way out of depression.

There are some who pick at food constantly when depressed, but the truly depleted person's stomach often objects even to the thought of food. Depletion is a biochemical disturbance, so it is essential to take the right nourishment while trying to recover. Therefore I suggest you discuss a vitamin supplement—and if necessary additional iron—with your doctor. One should not take iron as a habit. Your doctor will tell you whether you need it. If you have only been picking at food, you probably do.

A LOW-GRADE GUM INFECTION

With depletion, one's mouth may have an objectionable taste, which lessens appetite. This may be due to a low-grade gum infection or pockets of infection between teeth. Treatment with dental powder can bring quick relief, even help restore appetite.

A depleted person is sometimes deficient in calcium, and this is best taken as milk. At least a pint of milk should be drunk daily. If you feel you cannot take too much solid food, do not forget the egg flip made with sugar and a few drops of flavoring essence.

REFLECTING THE ENVIRONMENT

Some people can be depressed at home and yet on going away can snap out of the depression quickly, only to find depression descending at the mere thought of returning home. When emotional reserves are low, mood can respond surprisingly quickly to environment. When one is away from home, there is stimulation, and spirits rise accordingly. It is almost as if this person is a mirror in which the environment reflects itself, so that he or she feels quite different while away—not even tired. A woman like this needs a change in the home routine. Even a job for a few half days weekly can work wonders. The days at home are then grasped as an opportunity to get necessary work done and are no longer a stretch of boredom to be somehow lived through. Brightening up the kitchen helps; so much time is spent there.

Working away from home, if it can be managed (I have not forgotten I am speaking to some for whom leaving home is difficult) also opens new tracts of thought, even if it is only disapproval of the office receptionist's new hairstyle. If you are agoraphobic, somehow make the effort to bring a little change into your life. At least think in terms of remediable depletion and not of depression.

So:

- Think of yourself as temporarily depleted rather than depressed
- Your emotional battery will gradually recharge itself if you give it the chance.
- Wait as optimistically as you can manage.

- Everything cannot suddenly seem interesting.
- Trust in the miracle restored vitality will bring.

CHANGE OF LIFE

So much has been written about the menopause that it may seem unnecessary for me to mention it here; however, many women have asked if and how it can affect a nervously ill person when they are trying to recover the way I teach them. I can answer this question simply. The menopause may have no noticeable effect, or it may make emotional reaction (already exaggerated by sensitization) more easily aroused. You will notice I have not said it will make the reaction more exaggerated. "More easily aroused" is the crux of the matter. One point I wish to stress: Hot flushes are not the prerogative of the menopause. They may come to any of us at any time, especially in hot weather, so do not think a hot flush or two is heralding the "change."

Old wives have hair-raising tales to tell of the "change of life," but when pinned down to facts, one often finds they themselves did not have such a bad time; they merely knew a woman who did. Most busy women pass through the menopause with little disturbance. One doctor told me it was the only time in winter she could go to bed comfortably without a hot-water bottle. Even so, too frequent hot flushes can disturb even a busy person. One's doctor can break the cycle of hot flushes with hormone tablets. These should be taken as a restricted course and gradually diminished. Taking too many courses is not wise, as it only delays the menopause and may start uterine bleeding, which can be a nuisance. One can never be sure the bleeding is caused by the tablets, so the unlucky sufferer may have to go through several tests unnecessarily before the innocence of the bleeding is established. Although ovaries gradually stop functioning (and this is the basis of the menopause) ·ther glands adjust the hormone balance. Taking too much artificial ovarian hormone interferes with adjustment. Acceptance is once more the safest course. It would be, wouldn't it?

The more easily aroused emotional response can confuse a nervously ill person, whose emotions are easily enough aroused, goodness knows. Tears and exasperation are already too near the surface; panic flashes too easily. Also, this expensive use of emotion may weaken the emotional battery, and so the nervously ill person (or even the non–nervously ill) may, during the menopause, find herself easily depressed. Understanding why this happens and that it will pass does help. Occasionally some women have a few flushes ten years after their true menopause. We call this the little menopause. It passes quickly and has more curiosity value than importance.

Far too much is made of the menopause. It is a natural event that saves women from bearing children at an age when to do so would be dangerous. The term "change of life" should be abolished—if one knew how to abolish a term. This aspect of a woman's life simply changes to become more comfortable each month. One should, of course, keep an eye on the bathroom scales at this time. This is the time when extra pounds can creep on insidiously and weight needs watching. Also, do not be tempted to throw off a jacket or the bedclothes during a flush. Too many middle-aged chronic bronchitics owe their chronic illness to this habit. See the flush through, and you will gradually cool down. Another "see through"! How often this principle must be applied.

Salt and water retention three or four days before a menstrual period can physically and nervously disturb some women. Tablets can be prescribed to eliminate excess fluid and warning given to avoid salty foods and too many cups of coffee (too much fluid) during the premenstrual days.

THE SMALL COFFEE SHOP

I recently received the following letter:

After receiving the fifth journal, I decided to write about my progress and my hang-up. My general practitioner is very happy with what I have done. I am pleased also. He saw me through twelve years of not being able to do anything, and he felt helpless, as I could not follow his advice. I was too terrified to try. Then I bought your records, book, and now journals. The records are my salvation. They gave me just that something to get me going—also the fact that you said I could do it. I've had pretty strong setbacks; at one point I thought I was right back at my very worst, but I pulled out. However, I have a feeling of "What now?" as if maybe I'm cured, although I know I'm not, as you will see as you read on. I just don't get the elated feelings I used to when I did things, also no enthusiasm. Maybe I feel no challenge? I'm even working for the first time in twenty-two years. I rather think I am almost at a cured point. I could be feeling normal and not recognize it. After being anxious for twelve years, I believe I've forgotten what it is like to feel normal.

I hope you can understand what I am trying to say, although I cannot quite put it into writing. For example, this is one of my frustrating hang-ups: After going through a week of hell anticipating a hockey game, *the* night came, and I went without any of the fearful feelings I had had previously. Crowds bother me as a rule, but there were 13,000 people at that game, and except for slight dizziness, I had no anxious feelings. I was happy, but I did not get that elated feeling I thought I should have had.

I can do this, and yet in a small coffee shop I still

have an awful time. There are other small things left I cannot do. This is what is so puzzling. I don't seem able to handle a small coffee shop. I've been practicing for three months, at least once a week. I try different shops in different areas but always have a bad time of it. I have not tried having dinner out, as I was hoping to do this gradually, step by step, starting with the coffee shop. I've said, "Come and do your worst!" but I am still happy to get away. I've heard others express the same thing. I wonder if going all the way into a crowded restaurant would help at this point? I just do not know.

YOU CAN'T EAT YOUR CAKE AND HAVE IT TOO

I am sure this letter illustrates the way many of you may be now feeling. Elation, the stimulator in the early stages, must go as one gets used to doing things not done before. One cannot expect to continue feeling elated. How could elation possibly last? Satisfaction may continue to come, but such an acute emotion as elation is a rare visitor to any of us. No non–nervously ill person feels elated because he or she can sit through a hockey match; so when no longer elated, you are coming up well to being like other people. You are beginning to take doing the difficult for granted. This is good. It was so wonderful feeling thrilled after so many years of suffering, but you cannot eat your cake and have it too! There may be odd moments of elation from time to time, when it may suddenly dawn on you that this is actually *you sitting among all these people;* but unfortunately, such a sudden realization is often followed by memory stirring the embers of your illness, and on comes panic again. That is only to be expected. So pass right through it.

You might ask: "If this woman can manage the hockey game so well, why does she still have to suffer so much beforehand?" The answer is simple. She is not certain she can manage well. She has not managed well often enough yet to dull the edge of anxious anticipation. More "doing" is still the answer, even if without elation.

Also, waiting the week before the game reminds her so much of all the other outings anticipated in misery, that it recalls misery; but once she is at the game, she is reminded of the other more recent occasions when the doing has been successful, and this carries her through the ordeal. When she was ill and seldom went out, anticipation always meant dread, tension, fear of almost certain failure, and this is why it continues to bring such a buildup. The sufferer knows every minute of it only too well. That week of dreaded anticipation was not a "hang-up"; it was normal under the circumstances. It will be some time before this woman can take a hockey game in her stride, without thinking anxiously about it beforehand.

"TENDER-HANDED STROKE A NETTLE"

Now for the second section of the letter, about the coffee shop. This is a good example of "Tender-handed stroke a nettle, and it stings you for your pains." The writer has been making the old mistake of trying to cope with a special situation and not with herself (rather like the person who can drive anywhere, even fly to Europe, and yet finds walking up her own street difficult). She asks whether it would be better if she were to go to a crowded restaurant. In other words, by doing a big thing she dreads, would sitting in the smaller shop seem easier?

It might, but it might not. It would seem easier only if she were convinced it no longer meant any special effort. She would have to convince herself very successfully of this. I think, though, she would go to the coffee shop in such a state of "Will I be able to do it now?" that she would be in worse suspense than before. So much depends on attitude, and when one is susceptible to flashing emotion, the right attitude is hard to maintain—the old flash knows its way around every corner. In those little shops she has suffered so much that the memories are all there waiting for her. While she thinks in terms of a place to be coped with, she could always be afraid of a small coffee shop—or any small shop—however well she managed a crowded restaurant. In a little coffee shop this woman is still withdrawing from the feelings she dislikes so much. And she wonders why they should come there, when they did not come at the hockey game. She says, "Come and do your worst!" but she does not really mean this. She means, "Come quickly and do your worst and get it over with so I can get out of here. And when you do your worst, do not be too severe, please!"

THAT MOMENT OF PANIC-CRISIS

That is not good enough. She must regard a small coffee shop as a place in which she has an opportunity to face the ultimate (that moment of panic-crisis) until it no longer matters. It is still the moment, not the place. It does not matter where she has "the moment"; it is coping with herself at that moment that matters.

The writer of that letter still has to learn the trick of going toward panic with utter acceptance until she passes to the other side of panic. A little shop now seems more frightening because she is more exposed to close scrutiny, closer to those around her, more afraid of being noticed if she should "make a fool" of herself. At a crowded game, even in a crowded restaurant, she might feel bewildered by the noise and so on, but at the same time she is less conspicuous among so many and is therefore possibly less vulnerable to her fears (especially if she managed to get a seat near an exit). She is afraid of the same old fears, however, not the coffee shop. Onward, Christian soldier, into the coffe shop, *but withdraw from nothing*, and don't hope to get i over with quickly. Also, go more often than once weekly. *See it through, again and again*, in as relaxed a way as you can manage. As you do this, say to yourself, "Less tension, less adrenaline, and some day less panic." This is a physiological fact. Rely on it. Your body does, so why not you? I know your body gets the message in reverse—"More tension, more adrenaline, more panic"—and responds to this. Try giving it the opposite message, the right one. The same physiological rules will apply but perhaps not obviously at first because of sensitization. Understand this, and do not let the slowness of response bewilder you.

WHEN YOU ACCEPT THE ULTIMATE, YOU AUTOMATICALLY "LET GO"

You might say, "Doctor Weekes has given me two different kinds of advice: one, to let it come and do its worst and to face the ultimate until it no longer matters; and then the second, to relax and so reduce the adrenaline, which will then reduce the panic. Which am I to do?" There is no real difference between these two statements.

When you accept the ultimate, you automatically "let go" in attitude, and this brings the relaxation that lessens adrenaline and so eventually lessens panic. You do not get this relaxation unless you really "let go," though. You will never get it if you say, "Come and do your worst," with clenched teeth. So when this person goes into the coffee shop, she should go expecting the worst, be prepared to see it through as often as necessary with utter acceptance, and not be tricked into hurrying out of the shop as soon as possible. Halt! Go slowly; see the panic through. Stay there *until you are on the other side of panic. You can do it.* This is the hard way, *but it is the only permanent cure.* Because it is the hard way—as I mentioned in Journal 5—*it takes time.* So do not question the length of time it takes you to recover or think you are failing if you have not made much progress so far. If recovery is unduly slow, re-examine your attitude. You will find the clue to your failure there.

JOURNAL 7: Touching the Stars, What Is Reality?, Take Yourself by the Hand

TOUCHING THE STARS

As usual, this journal is for those still trying to get well, especially those who consider themselves unsuccessful so far. "Unsuccessful" is a misleading word. Some of you are tempted to apply it to yourselves when in a setback. Indeed, you may be tempted to think of yourselves as utter failures at this time and be thinking seriously of searching for some easier treatment. And yet if you look back to the time before you read my book and journals and compare yourself with the person you then were, very few of you will find you have been entirely unsuccessful all the time.

As one reader put it, "I touched the stars, but I can't do it again, and I can't believe I ever did it!" This woman had, after weeks of apprehension, vacationed successfully in Switzerland. She had even floated past the staggering realization that the Atlantic Ocean lay between her and home, only to find that on returning, the old fears flooded back all too quickly. And, of course, they seemed so much worse after tasting that wonderful freedom while away.

Stars, because they are stars, can only be touched rarely. To feel one can grasp and hold the stars, one must have frequent opportunity to practice doing so, and that is seldom available in an everyday program. Opportunity to practice my teaching is there in your own city, town, or suburb, but how humdrum it seems in comparison to the excitement, the variety, the beauty, of that successful journey away from home.

Coming back to the familiar brings so many small shocks. Nothing is more spirit-crushing than hearing the washing machine grinding noisily away cleaning the clothes you took on vacation, as if nothing unusual had happened. One can almost hear it say, "Come out of that dream, madam, and listen to me. I'm the one you must live with now, not those mountains, those lovely breakfasts by the lake. Wake up! It's time to switch me to spin-drier!"

THE VACATION BALLOON BURSTS

It helps if one realizes that the non–nervously ill person may also go through a similar experience of seeing the vacation balloon burst. Ecstasy is only ecstasy because it is short-lived, so do not lament if you cannot believe you ever touched a star, cannot believe you really did accomplish some outstanding feat. And don't be surprised if, despite the experience, you may feel you have made no progress when you return and may even seem unable to cope with the simpler tasks you managed well before going away. You will never lose what you have gained if you give yourself time to settle in and do not prolong the process by revolting against it. Don't let shock, surprise, or disappointment throw you completely off your stride. Once again, let the first shock pass, and you will slowly gather the harvest of success you planted when you touched the stars. Reading about vacationing in Switzerland may be tantalizing to those who haven't yet "made" the town center or the shops, but so many of you did go abroad on vacation after years of being housebound and wrote lamenting about the difficulty of homecoming that I thought I should mention it.

WHAT IS REALITY?

The feelings of a nervously ill person are important to him most of the time. This does not mean he is necessarily selfish or egotistical. He is simply so bewildered by his illness that he feels unable to be interested in other people, even in his family. He would like to care. A mother would truly like to *feel* love for her husband and children, but her detachment can be so great she becomes convinced she does not love them any more.

Emotions can always be deceptive, and in nervous illness *the emotions of the moment* dominate other feelings. For example a husband's failure to say the right thing at the right moment seems more important than the years of companionship. One woman said, "I know I must love my husband deep down inside me, but I can feel only exasperation at his actions and criticism." Unknowingly, this exasperation may be mixed with envy because the husband can do so casually what the wife so desperately wants to do. What is more, the doing is so easy for him that he cannot understand why it is not as easy for her.

THE SURFACE WAVES MAKE SO MUCH MORE FUSS

In her report a woman described the upsetting, even fearful, thoughts she had about her children. If only she knew how many mothers write about this, she would not think herself the monster she now does. I mention this particular fear so often in my book *Hope and Help for Your Nerves*, that I am surprised to be questioned again about it. I wonder if this woman has read the book or listened to my records, because she went on to say, "I am trying desperately to put the thoughts out of my mind." *This is the very thing I advise against doing.* The more desperately she tries to forget, the more imprinted the ideas will become. This is a normal physiological process.

Once more I stress that so much nervous illness is simply normal physiological process exaggerated, and therefore one cannot blot it out completely; one can only reduce it to normal intensity. She must let her thoughts come, as is their habit, but she must understand they are only thoughts and try to not be too impressed by them. They are like the surface waves, not the deep current, and it is the deep current that helps carry the ship along. Unfortunately, the surface waves make so much more fuss than the deep current and therefore seem so much more important. These frightening thoughts bring no truthful message, however forceful and real they may seem. They bring a message only of habit and fear, and these are not reality.

Reality is rarely the feeling of the moment. The feelings of the moment change with attitude, and reality is too deeply implanted to change readily with attitude. It survives the feelings of the moment, but how uncomfortable and convincingly real those momentary feelings can be to the nervously ill person. Don't be bluffed by frightening or negative feelings of the moment. Try to release them, let them go, float past them. They are not reality.

Some of you will not grasp the full meaning of what I write here or have written in other journals until you actually experience it. Then you will reread with interest and understanding. You may be surprised how much in the book and journals strikes you with new meaning when you reread them from time to time. Therefore, I risk repeating myself, and I will stress once more certain advice that is especially helpful.

1. Setbacks are so often memory and habit working together. Very rarely can one recover without them, so do not think you have "slipped right back" each time you happen to have a setback. Use the same method you used to come out of your illness. The more often you apply it, the more readily it will work.

2. Be consoled: The more improvement you have made, the more frustrating setback may seem, so do not let a particularly severe setback discourage you too much. A woman in San Francisco said jokingly, "I must be recovering, doctor, because I'm having my worst setback!" Two months later she was able to travel to Paris for the first time in years.

3. Physical illness, especially that frequent visitor influenza, can so deplete you that the old symptoms of nervous stress return or threaten to return. Most of you know that apprehensive feeling when the old dreaded sensations hover and you are afraid they will really arrive. Let them hover; do not try to push them away, or run away from them—at the same time looking over your shoulder to see if they have really gone!

I know how possible it may all seem on Monday and yet how impossible on Tuesday. Strange, how all the possible Mondays may still fail to convince you when one impossible Tuesday comes along. Try to be patient through impossible Tuesday—even through physical illness—and trust in nature to repair the damage, with a doctor's help if necessary.

4. Recovery may be so new and strange that it is as if you have lost something you must find again. This something is your illness. So do not be surprised if when you are most successful, the very strangeness of success makes you feel odd. Don't be surprised if this oddness reminds you so acutely of your illness that you are beguiled into thinking you are ill again. It is almost as if you cannot tolerate recovery.

You will eventually feel at ease with success when enough of it robs it of strangeness. So pass through every such experience until it no longer surprises and upsets you.

5. Wanting everything one minute and nothing the next is one of the most tantalizing aspects of depletion. Also, you may think yourself capable of doing everything one

minute and then incapable of doing anything the next. This too is usual. Is it any wonder that I keep advising acceptance and warning against trying to delve for reasons for "this" or "that"?

6. I know that feelings often depend on circumstances and that when these change, feelings automatically improve. There is the other side of the coin, however, and this is not appreciated as much as it should be. When feelings are less intense, circumstances seem less overwhelming. The proof of this lies in the effect tranquilizers may have. After tranquilization the impossible may seem so much more possible. So try to not be too impressed even by circumstances. By going toward them willingly, you lessen tension, and problems may not seem so insurmountable.

7. The way to recovery is the same for most of you. Blasters come when least expected. Pass through. Pass through. *Always pass through to the other side*, and never run away. Running away is such a waste of time because once you have started to recover by using the method advised in these journals, you will always turn back and tackle that obstacle again. Wait. Gather breath for a new advance. It may take time and many changes of mind, but eventually you will do it. Some who have discarded my advice and have tried other methods have written, saying that after a while they find themselves back in square one, using the book and journal once more.

Indeed, many have said they carry the journal wherever they go. This conjures up such a picture of tattered pages among lipstick, purse, and tissues and of shaking hands rejecting page after page while frantically searching for a special passage that I include here a short article that can be conveniently carried and which will be especially helpful when you are trying to travel away from home. It was originally made as a ten-minute long-playing recording.

Again, there will be repetition, but for those who still need help, repetition is treatment. Goodness knows that through fear and habit, some of you repeat the wrong advice to yourselves often enough. Repeating the right advice—hearing it again and again—is essential. Don't think, "I know that," and pass it by. It is not enough to just "know" it in your head. *You must really feel it in your heart.* Do you really feel it?

TAKE YOURSELF BY THE HAND

If you are suffering from fear of leaving the safety of home, you probably had an experience in the past which upset you to an exaggerated degree and, as I have already explained, sensitized you. So many women say, "It all started after the birth of my last baby."

If like this, you are not really afraid of open spaces, even of the supermarket. You know perfectly well that if you go to the corner store, the grocer won't shoot you and the houses won't topple on you. You know none of these will happen to you. So what are you afraid of? You are afraid of the feelings that arise within you when in these situations, feelings that seem to overwhelm you, so that you seem unable to think clearly while they are present. You do not trust yourself while you are like this, and this is why you are afraid to go out alone.

I will now take you out with me, step by step; and as we go, I will explain exactly what happens, why it happens, and what to do about it. Are you ready? Good.

But look at you! Before we've even opened the front door, you have tensed yourself like a violin string tightly screwed. You thought, "Oh, my goodness! What's going to happen now?" If one plucks a taut string, it responds by vibrating, whereas a slack string does not. By tensing your body, you have made it an instrument on which your fears can play a painful tune, and you have done this before you even put one foot outside the door. *This is your first mistake.*

Instead of tensing your body in anticipation of what might happen, let it go, slacken it, release it. Slacken those strings. The worst that can happen out there in the street, in those shops, is that you let yourself become frightened. I know how severe that fright can be, but if you release as much tension as possible and are prepared to accept what happens, prepared to surrender yourself to it, it won't be quite so overwhelming. Surrender; accept. Slacken those strings. Take a slow breath; let it out gently. Have you gotten the idea? (Have you really gotten the idea?) Good.

HERE COMES MRS. X

We are off—but oh my goodness, here comes Mrs. X from down the street! What are you going to do about her? You advance toward her with your heart in your mouth. You can feel your heart thumping in your throat, banging in your chest. Your neighbor's heart is also beating quickly, though, perhaps just as quickly as yours. She is intrigued because she hasn't seen you out alone for months. Then why should your heart's quick beating be so specially frightening, so particularly uncomfortable? Yours is so upsetting because your sensitized nerves are recording and amplifying each beat. Does it really matter if you feel your heart beating? It doesn't matter in the least. It certainly doesn't harm your heart. So don't be afraid to feel your heart pounding while you talk to Mrs. X.

She is settling in for a good old gossip. What if she were to continue for another ten minutes, half an hour? You tremble at the thought and think, "I can't stand it. I'll make a fool of myself. She'll notice!"

Now I whisper, "Take your hand off that screw. Let your body slacken. Loosen. Loosen. Take a deep breath, let it out slowly, and surrender completely to listening to Mrs. X. She'll eventually stop."

You hear me. You hesitate and then release the tension just a little, and strangely enough, standing there does not seem quite so difficult. You even feel a little pleased with yourself. And so you should be because you have discovered something very important. You've learned Mrs. X is not upsetting you, as you thought; you were upsetting yourself. *It was your hand tightening that screw, not hers.*

We are off down the street again. You feel a little better. You made it! Now you must cross the main road, however, and just when you need your legs most, they suddenly turn to jelly. Those old jelly legs. Did I say suddenly? It did not happen quite as suddenly as you thought. As you approached the main road, you became frightened again, and fear released that old enemy adrenaline, which gave you the jelly legs. The effect will gradually pass if you do not stay frightened by it and so add more adrenaline, but you do not understand this and stand rooted to the pavement, sure your legs will never carry you across.

JELLY LEGS WILL STILL GET YOU THERE

Here again I whisper, "Jelly legs will still get you there if you will let them. It is only a feeling, not a true muscular weakness. Don't be bluffed by jelly legs. Don't add more adrenaline by being afraid of them. Let them wobble. They can carry you across the street whether they wobble or not. And don't think you must hold tensely onto yourself to keep yourself from collapsing. *It's the holding on that exhausts, not the letting go.* So let your legs wobble. It's only a feeling, not a true muscular weakness."

You crossed the road. You made it. By now you are not quite so impressed by the tricks your body has been playing on you. When you realize this, you somehow feel charged with new strength. Wait! You have forgotten the shop!

There may be half a dozen neighbors waiting to talk in there! You may even have to wait in line!

In a flash you turn on all screws at once and give yourself the full fear treatment. It is as if you have made no progress at all—and just when you thought you were beginning to get the right idea. While you look at the shop in despair, your body seems to sway, the street to swirl, the buildings to topple, everything goes blurred. You clutch at a lamppost to steady yourself. How are we going to explain this one? *This* is a beauty!

It is explained very simply. Severe tension disturbs co-ordination between your muscles and the balancing apparatus, and this apparatus receives the wrong messages. So the building seem to topple, and you feel unsteady. Also, fear dilates your pupils, and vision therefore seems blurred. This is so frightening you withdraw from it; you let it overwhelm you. It is only the same old tricks in disguise, though, the same old turn of the screw. And as usual you turned it yourself.

LET THE STORM PASS

Wait! Let the storm pass. Let the effects of adrenaline pass. Even at the climax of your fears, surrender and accept. At the very moment when your feelings seem to engulf you, that is the moment above all when you must surrender and accept. No more "oh, my goodnesses," no more "what ifs."

If you do this, you will find you will keep the grip on yourself you previously lost. If you go forward, however hesitantly, with understanding of what is happening, ready to accept all the tricks your fears may play upon you, your reactions will gradually calm. You won't have to try walking as far as the corner store one week and into town the next until you finally graduate to the supermarket. You will find peace in the middle of the town square, *because you take your cure with you, wherever you might be.*

Just as you read this advice, say it to yourself again and again when you are out until you make it part of yourself. It will never fail you if you follow it and follow it until you learn to take yourself by the hand, until you are your own guide, your own strength.

A letter from a woman:

All the fears and sudden panic you speak about have been mine for years except that I have never given way to confining myself to the house. But as you point out in your bulletins, in spite of the help your book gave me, I continued to be plagued by them, though I am now trying to accept rather than fight them.

Last November, a friend agreed to go with me on a cruise to the Canary Islands. I had not thought anyone would want to go anywhere with me.

From the time of booking, I seemed less physically well than usual—pains in my middle, diarrhea—and I was obliged to go to my doctor. He gave me various remedies, but the main advice was to step up my tranquilizers a little until I got going. Even the day before we sailed, I felt I could not go, and only a good talking to from my doctor and fear of disappointing my friend made me pack and go.

So with Avomine against seasickness and three tranquilizers a day for about three days, I went. I was not seasick, and not once did I panic. I found myself talking happily to many passengers and actually played two piano solos in the ship's concert. I took your bulletins and read them in bed occasionally. If we did not get the sun we hoped for, I feel I have gained my old confidence in myself, which matters more than anything.

I have no doubt that when I next plan a vacation, even if it is only in the United States, I shall struggle with the same fears and have the same uncomfortable physical aches and pains, but I hope that after this experience I shall not be such a coward again. I am grateful to my doctor for the patience he showed me and to the journals for showing people like me you don't think us the fools we often think we are.

The following is an especially interesting report:

Some of you may feel, as I did at one time, that maybe other people may benefit from Dr. Weekes's teaching but that you are too much of a coward to manage it. May I tell you of my experience and how I realized that no matter how cowardly you are, it works?

Just recently, I had the misfortune—or as it happened in the end, the fortune—to be a police witness at a trial. When I was told one Friday that I would have to appear as a witness on the following Monday at court, I spent the whole weekend working myself up until I was sure I could not go. When you consider that I cannot go out alone at all, I think you will realize the worries I had.

The police were to call and collect my husband and me by car, and the journey there and back was thirty-nine miles. We were to be there at 10:30 A.M. As most of you know, waiting is for many of us one of the worst things.

The jury was not sworn in until 12:45 P.M. Then the court adjourned for lunch. My husband had gone for a walk, and I was left alone in this large building. Before I left home, I had slipped a copy of one of the journals into my handbag, just in case. By relaxing and following exactly in my mind what I had read so many times in the journals, I was able to find the ladies' room. When my husband returned, I was back in the main hall, having quite calmly combed my hair and generally freshened up. We went up in the elevator to the cafeteria and had lunch.

At 2 P.M. I was taken into the courtroom. This was the real test. It was followed by forty minutes of grueling questioning on the witness stand. I did not feel one ounce of fear.

How could I, such a dreadful coward, have done this? It was just by remembering what Dr. Weekes had said. I did not even take the journal from my handbag. After all that time waiting, plus the forty minutes' questioning when I had to go it alone, I feel a new person. So if you are like me, a real coward, listen to the words written in each journal, and take heart. It works; it really does.

Once again, I assure you that if you are prepared to do your part, you can definitely be cured. I would not spend so much time and effort writing these journals if I did not know this. I look forward to a better understanding of agoraphobia and of the anxiety state in general in the future, and consequently to improved treatment. This must come, and an increasing number of therapists are reading these journals and listening to the records.

TAKING THE FIRST STEPS

When first reading these journals, you may feel encouraged to practice as advised and yet may be afraid to take the first step. If you are afraid in this way, it is usually for one or more reasons:

1. You have been ill so long that you think you are beyond help.

2. You do not trust yourself to try again. You have tried in so many different ways to recover in the past and have—as you think—let yourself down so badly that you haven't the heart to begin again.

3. You understand what I advise but panic so easily

that despite your best efforts, you seem to wilt before each onslaught.

4. You feel so emotionally, mentally, and physically weary that you shrink from taking the first steps. Those first steps open up such a vista of effort that you quail before it.

You Think You Have Been Too Ill to Recover Now

First, understand that no outside force is doing this to you. Your body is simply responding to the way you think. It may be sensitized, but although sensitization seems to come from the depths of your being, it is really superficial and can be healed. This healing power is in each of us. You have it as much as anyone else; you are simply standing in its way. Your body is not irrevocably altered physiologically by your illness. If you have been ill for years (and I have known people nervously disturbed for most of their lives), it means only that the habit of nervous illness will be strongly entrenched and that memory will be discouraging. You have the power to accept and discount these, however. You still have the power of free will *through acceptance,* although it may seem as if you have not. You have it.

Although a nervously ill person may find peace and understanding while with his doctor, however, he (as previously mentioned) may have forgotten most of the good advice a few hours later because his tired mind forgets so easily. This makes taking the first steps especially difficult. Hence I record for my patients an interview to encourage taking first steps, to encourage getting themselves moving. Just as the nervous person has bombarded himself with defeatist suggestions over the past months, now he can bombard himself with a doctor's constructive advice on a tape recording (or on long-playing records if a tape is not available—see the footnote on p. 70 for information on obtaining these records) until it becomes so much a part of himself that he *feels* its meaning strongly enough to find the courage to set off. I stress again: There is, in my opinion and experience, no such thing as a chronic anxiety state that cannot be cured if the sufferer understands what is needed of him and is willing to play his part.

You Do Not Trust Yourself

It doesn't matter if you don't trust yourself. I am not asking you to. I ask you only to try to understand the advice I give and trust *it*. However big a coward you may think yourself now, *the advice still works*. You do not have to cure yourself; you let your body do that. You simply stand aside, out of the way, by adding as little *second* fear as possible—resisting adding "oh, my goodness" and "what if." Trust your body to heal itself while you practice the teaching here. It has responded faithfully to the wrong messages you have been sending it; it will respond just as faithfully to the right ones—although more reluctantly at first.

You Understand, but Fear Flashes So Fiercely You Wilt before It

You may have to accept much flashing fear for the time being. You probably feel that when panic strikes, you cannot think at all, so that practicing "going with it" seems impossible. However severe the panic, if you watch yourself closely, you will discover that you can think, even if the wrong thoughts. Practicing going with, and not shrinking from, fear is like learning to ride a bicycle. There is a certain amount of falling off before you finally learn to ride, but unless you pick yourself up each time and try again, you never learn. Never forget that *failure is not finality*.

To teach a patient a practical way to deal with his fear, I press my hand hard against his chest and ask him to move forward against the pressure. As he strains forward, I point out that this is the tense way he has been reacting to fear. I then ask him to stretch his arms out before him and move them as if swimming forward in deep, cool water. Usually I can feel some of the tension relax immediately.

Some people so dislike the thought of water that they avoid bathing, even washing their hair. To them I suggest the feeling of drifting forward on a cloud. This, or thinking of swimming forward in deep, cool water, is not as foolish as it may sound. It brings a feeling of release and gives something positive and helpful to do at a critical moment when otherwise one would probably withdraw tensely in defeat. So when you take those first steps, take them "in deep, cool water" or in any other relaxed way (floating forward) you care to imagine.

You Think You Haven't the Strength to Take That First Step

In my earlier book I described a woman who, "exhausted" by her nerves, had been more or less confined to a couch for months, believing she was too weak to stand for long. As treatment I urged her immediately to begin painting the woodwork on the back porch. Against her will and to her husband's amazement, she began. In a few days she was painting with interest.

So much nervous weakness is encouraged by loss of confidence in what one's body can do. Remember that this weakness is not true organic muscular weakness, although it may feel like it, so don't let it keep you on a couch. Your muscles grow stronger only as you use them. Once more I stress that you should be examined by your doctor and assured your weakness is nervous. If you have the slightest urge to practice what I advise, encourage it by making the effort to take that first step—however long you may have been ill, however much you may distrust yourself, however afraid you may be, however tired you think you are.

JOURNAL 8: The Importance of Habit—The Forbidden Handbag, The First Hurdle, An Agoraphobic Woman Describes Her Journey to Recovery

I first wish to talk yet again about coping with setback. So many doctors lose heart when trying to help their patients cope with setback. And yet if doctor and patient can understand and bear with setback, recovery is the prize.

Some of you have had moments, even weeks, when you have felt—to quote one woman—you could "tackle anything" and then have had a setback, which—to quote the same woman—"makes everything very ugly again." She also adds:

I still find myself shrinking from my thoughts; at the same time I almost see things in their right proportion, only to slip back into the old habits once more. I'm having a setback at present after a fairly good period. I feel terribly disappointed, and yet I know I'll build up slowly again.

For instance, today I had a few moments when I actually lost my fear of my main phobia. It was the best moment in that direction. One learns an awful lot from breakdown. I look forward to the time when I can see it all in the right light. The intelligent part of me knows it is quite ridiculous, but fear seems always to hold the upper hand.

THE IMPORTANCE OF HABIT—THE FORBIDDEN HANDBAG

I would like you to appreciate the importance of the word "habit" because so much of your illness is bound up in that word. Fear of this or that *is your habit*. This is why you seem to have things sorted out and to see them clearly, without fear, for a while and then lose that reasonable glimpse. It is not so much that fear alone comes back as that *the habit of fear reasserts itself*. When you appreciate the full meaning of habit, you will understand why setbacks come and why your progress seems to include so much going backward, so much slipping back into old habits—rather like climbing a greased pole.

A woman carries her handbag everywhere. Suppose she were told that she must never carry one, that she must go empty-handed. Do you really believe she would immediately adapt herself to not carrying a handbag and feel comfortable when going out? For months she would feel lost and would make the gesture of looking for it before leaving home, make the gesture·many times in many different places to see if she had it with her. Even months after she had thought herself adjusted to being without her bag, she could suddenly find herself automatically groping for it.

Recovering from nervous illness is like this. Should you lose your fear for a while, the "you behind you" (you know the "you" I mean) is so used to being afraid that from habit it will go looking for your fear to present it to you again. If you could then think, "This is only the return of the lost handbag!" and go forward through the fear, you would once more come out into the clearing.

In my book *Hope and Help for Your Nerves* I talk about the curtain lifting and then descending again. Also,

I say, "If you can but glimpse for a few moments daily without fear, you will have made a beginning. With practice you will glimpse more readily and hold the glimpse for longer and longer until it is the final established point of view. Then you will be at peace."

Glimpsing is a frustrating, painful process, *but it is part of recovery.* So do not think of those persistent efforts of the "you behind you" as failure; try to see them as an inevitable part of getting well. You are still improving even when being presented with the forbidden handbag. Habit dies hard, but in time it does die if you see it through its violent protestations.

The First Hurdle

The following letter is from an agoraphobic woman who kept herself ill by misunderstanding and mismanagement. I analyze in detail certain sentences, which I have put in italics:

I am trying to follow the advice in your book, but *I can't get over the first hurdle.* My trouble came on after a lengthy illness, when I began to have panicky feelings when out of doors. You say in your book to relax and take deep breaths, etc., but this is my main trouble, *I just can't take a deep breath. I gasp and gulp and feel myself suffocating, which brings on more fear.*

You also say "let time pass," but I have been ill so long *I must get better soon.* Life is passing me by, and I am getting nowhere. *I feel such a coward and such a failure. I used to be able to make myself do things I was afraid of, but now all my willpower is gone.*

If only I could get out again without fear, I could get my old job back. Please, *how can I control these panic spasms when I try to go out?* If I was all right when I went out, there would be nothing to fear, and

I could go. But now, feeling the way I do, I sometimes daren't even go to the street corner. If a gasping panic comes on, I have to be near home so that I can get back quickly. *I feel like I am going to faint and just have to run home.*

When this woman says, "I can't get over the first hurdle," she is trying to say she can't rid herself of enough fear to begin practicing my advice. She stresses this when she says, "If only I could get out again without fear." She will never go out without fear while she puts off going until she is without fear. She has waited in vain for years to be without fear. Waiting and watching so fearfully keeps her body always altered to respond in an exaggerated way, so she feels ordinary fear as panic. And the ground is well prepared for panic while it is feared so much. Her anxiety provides the adrenalin from which panic is made. When she said, "If only I could get out again without fear," she was really saying, "If only a magic wand would remove my fears!" This young woman is looking for a cure outside herself. She won't find it—not a lasting cure. She must be prepared to go out *the way she feels now* and not wait until she is unafraid.

She must not go tensely, hoping fear will not come. Fear will certainly come, so she must be prepared to be afraid but at the same time try to release as much tension as possible, if not in her body (this may seem impossible at this stage), at least in her attitude. Once again I stress that she must go toward fear, not shrink from it, and must be prepared to let it do its worst. Only when she has faced fear and managed to see it through in this way will she remove the underlying apprehension and tension which are creating the very fears she fears. A habit of fear can be broken only when it is faced with acceptance. Only then will moving about away from home—or any other dreaded experience—cease to be such an ordeal.

Once again I stress the difference between true accept-ance and just "putting up with." "Putting up with" means advancing and yet retreating at the same time. It means an attitude of "Hurry! Hurry! Get it over with quickly!"

When one is first attempting to face and accept fear, speed in taking those first steps only heightens tension. Faltering steps—and they are faltering steps, almost like a child's—should never be taken quickly. A moderate pace gives time to remember and practice what I teach. It gives time to collect the right attitude to panic—time to see how much one is frightening oneself. Speed encourages adding *second* fear and achieves nothing except defeat because speed means running away, although you may be actually heading in a forward direction. *You can defeat panic only by giving yourself time to work with it.*

So when you attempt to meet any situation you fear, *start slowly,* and continue at a moderate pace until the end; *go even more slowly when panic reaches its peak.* Hurrying is agitation, and agitation in a sensitized person sets the scene for panic.

Acceptance means a certain resignation, and resignation implies a certain peace. A hunted criminal who finally becomes resigned to his fate and gives himself up finds some peace. This is not unlike the feeling the nervously ill person feels when he finally decides to surrender to the worst fear can do—when he decides to accept and not fight.

"I just can't take a deep breath. I gasp and gulp and feel myself suffocating." Who wouldn't if they fought for breath the way she does? She will not suffocate, however, because her lungs will expand enough despite her efforts to thwart them. She *is* thwarting them with her tense struggle. She need not worry about taking a deep breath. Shallow breathing will do *if she punts with acceptance.* As the tension passes, her chest muscles relax and breath-ing becomes normal. Even if she gulps and gasps, she won't suffocate, because as already explained there is a breathing center in her brain which automatically controls her breathing in spite of her heroic efforts. Surely she has gulped and gasped often enough without suffocating to prove this to herself.

"I must get better soon." Once more she is creating tension by putting a time limit on recovery. How understandable this is, though. She has been ill so long that she is desperate. To be patient seems almost impossible, but impatience means more tension, more sensitization. She must try to be reconciled to giving as much time as necessary to recovery. Under the circumstances, in what better way could she spend her time than in working for recovery? She must surrender even to this.

"I feel such a coward and such a failure." Why should she? She has struggled heroically for years. Few understand how much she has struggled and suffered. She has failed only because she hasn't known how to succeed, not because she hasn't tried. Every line of her letter shows how she struggles bravely—but in the wrong way. Exhaustion and despair, not cowardice, have almost stopped her in her tracks.

"I used to be able to make myself do things I was afraid of, but now all my willpower is gone." One can almost feel the lashing she must have given herself. "My willpower is gone" is simply another way of saying, "I have so exhausted myself with fighting and getting nowhere that hope has gone." Who wouldn't be tired of tilting at such windmills? The majority of nervously ill people, including the most intelligent, seem naturally to take the wrong road and *fight* their illness. I hope by now you see the difference between fighting and accepting?

When one surrenders and accepts, going out or doing anything one is afraid of may at first continue to be grim. Indeed, in the beginning it may seem especially difficult because facing and accepting demands more energy than resting at home in defeat. The nervous person usually has so little reserves that she thinks she simply hasn't the strength to try to recover this way. As she learns to accept this temporary additional tiredness, the keen edge of panic gradually dulls just a little, and she builds strength and hope on this "little."

"How can I control these panic spasms?" She can't immediately, because she is sensitized, and she can't turn panic off like a tap. One can't expect to control directly a whipping flash that at times seems to come like an electric shock. The control is. *indirect,* and as I have explained so often, comes only by learning not to add panic to panic. Only in this way can she begin to desensitize herself until panic gradually grows less intense.

"I feel like I am going to faint and just have to run home." She feels she is going to faint, but she can still *run* home. If she can run back toward home without fainting, surely she could *walk* toward the shops instead? She is not running away from fainting. She is running away from the fear she will faint, *from the fear that makes her feel faint*. When she is headed toward home, her fear decreases, so naturally she feels less faint.

If she would practice walking forward in the way I have stressed so often in these journals, by letting her body do whatever it wants to—tremble if it must, feel weak if it must, *even faint if it feels like it* (this takes a lot of acceptance!)—she would find behind the trembling and the faintness the strength to move forward, however hesitatingly. *She would not faint.*

Each despairing statement in this letter was based on a misunderstanding that entrenched the writer more deeply in her illness. Surely it is time for her to try a new approach, directly opposite the one she has been using. Is not this the approach I teach?

An Agoraphobic Woman Describes Her Journey to Recovery

I am at last beginning to make some progress. As I found the early stages of recovery bewildering and believe this is not unusual, I thought others, struggling as I did, might be interested to read of my experience.

When I first read Dr. Weekes's book, I thought here at last was an explanation of how to cope with my illness because the more I studied her method, the more it seemed right. I agreed wholeheartedly that curing the state I was in was the important thing, and not trying to find an original cause. I never could understand how finding a cause hidden beneath twenty-eight years of suffering could help me now, even though most of the psychiatrists who had tried unsuccessfully to help me had thought so. To take myself in my own hands, regardless of the past, and not look for an outside cure to make recovery easy was a challenge I knew I must face at last if I was to recover.

Did I have the courage, the staying power? Could I do it? Had I been ill too long? Could I stay convinced this was the right way to recover, even if others tried to convince me it was not? Did I have all this? Others had managed, so why shouldn't I?

My immediate reaction to the explanation of sensitization and how panic occurs was one of relief and hope. I decided to try the basic theory of facing, accepting, floating, and letting time pass. I must say the thought of letting more time pass filled me with dismay, as half my life had gone in illness. However, I took off with some enthusiasm and achieved minor successes in moving about which I had not made in years. "Could it really be as easy as this?" I asked myself. Surely there must be more to recovery than taking off in a flash this way. I soon learned that for me, there was

—because the early elation passed, and I was back where I started.

I know now the first elation merely masked my fears. The real start had to come more slowly and not so emotionally. I studied Dr. Weekes's method until it became part of my thinking, so much so that one day I spontaneously took off in a bus and traveled a short distance from home. This was the first bus I had boarded in twenty years. I was excited, but when I reached home, I was so exhausted that I could not believe I had been near a bus.

For weeks this cycle repeated itself—minor successes followed by fatigue, but no real feeling of growing confidence. Each adventure seemed too great an ordeal to bring lasting confidence. But I could not lose the glimpse of success I had had when first doing these things. I had touched something I was unable to grasp and hold, *but I had touched it.*

I realized that although some could go out immediately and never look back after reading Dr. Weekes's book and listening to her records, others would find the method hard. I had to accept that I was one of these. I remembered her words, "Each recovers in his or her own time. Accept even that." Realizing this method would work for me only if I was willing to accept it fully and let the cure come from inside myself, in its own time, I accepted the time involved at last.

It was hard to think cure had to come from me, for I had always hoped for cure from an outside source. And yet however hard I found doing this by myself, a little voice inside me kept niggling, making me keep on course.

On one occasion after I had managed to travel some distance from home, everything seemed to recede, and I felt completely lost; I felt incapable of asking anyone to help me home or hail a taxi. This was different from flashing panic. However, remembering Dr. Weekes's method, I managed to think, "Meet this the same way as panic. Wait. Take it slowly." Finally I was able to hail a taxi. I realized that what I had suffered was no more than supertension and had to be met the same way as any other form of panic.

Progress still seemed a dream, although I was learning so much. I managed successfully one day and failed the next, was sure one day and despaired the next. I became desperate when I heard of fellow sufferers, also using Dr. Weekes's method, who were making quicker progress than I was. I suspected I might not have what it took to stay in the race.

At times my illness seemed a safer way of life; at least I knew where I stood, and it sometimes seemed better than being a perpetual emotional yo-yo, up one minute and down the next. But once I started, I could not give up.

A few days later I drove round Central Park on my own. Panic after panic flashed. When I returned home, I was so spent and upset I nearly vomited. This, I decided, was my last attempt. I would stop the whole thing now. But somehow I didn't feel the relief I expected. That wretched little voice kept niggling. Where had I gone wrong? Why had I failed?

Trembling in every limb (because I suspected that wretched little voice would make me try to do the trip again), I analyzed where I had made my mistakes. Suddenly I knew I had accepted nothing. I had tried to get through the trip at the fastest possible speed and had withdrawn from panic by *trying to blast my way through it*. My one thought had been, "Get home at all costs!"

I decided to drive round the park again and this time try to make a success out of failure. I would try to learn from my mistake. After a good dose of glucose

I set off very, very slowly, prepared to meet panic when it came and to try not to add *second* fear. On that first journey, I knew I had added so much *second* fear. At my special panic-spot I slowed down almost to a crawl. Of course, I panicked, but I saw the flash right through and kept going forward slowly but willingly with the car. I did not panic again. Don't ask me why, but I didn't. Three times I repeated this journey. I saw at last that recovery could begin to work only from actual experience and that that was why it must take time.

I now became almost obsessional in my desire to experiment with myself. I was afraid to let a day pass without doing something new. I thought that if I did, I would lose the progress I had made. This was a mistake because it led to more tiredness. I was trying too hard. I learnt to take even this aspect of recovery more sensibly. If I missed a day or two, I stopped whipping myself.

In spite of now feeling I am on the right track and in spite of feeling real hope, I am sometimes nervier than when I was in the shelter of my agoraphobia. This, Dr. Weekes explains, is because I am meeting situations I have avoided for years and am putting myself in the line of fire for further panic. It is obvious that the road to recovery may temporarily bring increased sensitization, and this makes one feel as if no progress has been made. However, if we repeat some of the earlier steps, we will find they are surprisingly easy. For example, the other day I found entering a big store alone effortless. This came as a surprise because I had formerly done so at great cost. This gave me hope.

Recovery sometimes makes me feel so unreal that I have to keep remembering Dr. Weekes's words, "A feeling of unreality during recovery is normal under the circumstances." To me, for twenty years my illness has been my reality, so I suppose it is only natural these new experiences should feel unreal. I do understand that only when "going it alone" is not a novelty will my changed way of life begin to feel real.

Setback, exhaustion, depression, panic—all seem part of failure. Yet I have learned that I cannot go forward without them. This is a hard lesson to learn because it is not easy to put oneself voluntarily into positions that may bring these feelings. Although I am only at the beginning of this road, I have had those moments of glimpsing which have brought me such hope that I feel that to turn back now would be impossible, and I fear going forward a little less.

LETTER FROM THE SAME WOMAN EIGHT MONTHS LATER

Since my last letter I have had to come through a severe setback following an operation. All went well during the first part of January. Driving around Central Park and going into a store held no more fear. Even on a bad day I could see the panic through and come out on the other side. To take a bus was an everyday occurrence. Also, there was a marked change in my attitude. I felt more positive as a person and was meeting domestic crises more calmly. This change was reflected in my work.

Could this be what I had waited for during these twenty-eight years? Would this glimpse really hold? Could I go further? Dare I be sure? My feet were only just touching firm ground, and I knew it. Then suddenly, for the first time in my life, I was faced with an operation. It couldn't have come at a worse time. If only I had had a little time to consolidate that glimpse. But things rarely work out that way. Indeed, no sooner was an operation decided on for me than my son had to have two, one following the other.

I had always had a dread of hospitals, especially of operations, and waiting for a bed was not easy. However, although because of physical illness I was no longer able to practice moving about, I did practice Dr. Weekes's teaching to help me through the waiting period. I also practiced it in the hospital. Those experiences I dreaded most—for example, the preoperative ritual—lost much of their dread when once I faced and accepted them. Looking back now, I am glad of the experience. I no longer fear the hospital so much.

But I wasn't going to be let off so easily. I had postoperative complications, and the journey home from the hospital showed me how sensitized I had become. Starting all over again while I felt so weak and sensitized seemed too much. I thought I was at the bottom of the ladder and couldn't imagine how I had ever managed to do what I had been doing before entering the hospital. I felt so exhausted I didn't even want to recover again. That was that.

I was making the mistake of being, to quote Dr. Weekes, "duped by my thinking." I was duped into thinking recovery from this physical illness depended entirely on my effort, when I felt incapable of making effort. Never having had an operation before, I did not know how much physical setback was to be expected, although my surgeon warned me of some of it. Having come through, I will never again be bluffed by the feelings that follow physical illness.

Despite myself, nature began to work. Gradually strength came back. I thought, "If I can come out of this, I'll never be so afraid of setback again." I took heart and decided to stop kicking against fate.

Gradually, as I felt stronger, the old urge to try once more returned. How much *had* I lost? The return was gradual. At one stage I hardly dared venture out alone. And just when I was picking up, I had an attack of such violent giddiness that I was nearly thrown to the floor. This was all I needed to finish me off. Small wonder I hesitated to start again because my cure lies in being able to drive my car alone. Driving in heavy New York traffic is sensitizing in itself, without the added fear of having another vertigo attack. However, I was reassured when a specialist told me nothing organic was wrong and that it was most unlikely I would have another attack.

Also, Dr. Weekes explained that unless I tried again, I would be left straddling two worlds—the world of agoraphobia and the world of recovery I had glimpsed so well. She was right. That glimpse was my undoing. I just had to go on.

Of course, I panicked. Noise, traffic—all seemed so much worse than before. But I understood this was to be expected in my condition, and I stopped watching my reactions so closely. I even had the sense to stop comparing what I could do now with what I could do in January—three months earlier.

Gradually I climbed back to some feeling of confidence as each achievement reminded me of those earlier efforts. I had not forgotten as much as I thought! Indeed, repeating some of the old experiences, like driving round Central Park, proved that the early foundation was there. I was soon to find I was now readier for harder undertakings, and that is how I am today.

I am now trying to work without any props. I used to think, "Well, I can always telephone home, and someone will come." But now I go off when no one is home. I made little practices at first. One day, with as little contemplation as possible, I went fifteen miles by car. It was a great moment. Don't envy me too much. It was not easy, and three days later I made a complete mess of the same journey. But I have learned one thing. I cannot stay happy when I fail. I have to go out again and correct my mistakes. As Dr. Weekes explains,

"Recovery lies in repeated doing until the memory of enough achievement replaces defeatist contemplation."

Believe me, I still have my full share of defeatist contemplation, especially at night, when with my head on the pillow it all seems impossible. But the next day somehow I'm at it again, and once I'm in the car, the doing takes over. I know that for complete recovery, the day must come when the umbilical cord between myself and outside support must be completely cut, and this is what I am working at now.

Although last summer brought much domestic strain to this woman, she has been able to consolidate the progress she had made with agoraphobia. She can now drive alone to the golf course, seven miles away, and play all day without needing someone near. She recently drove two hundred miles and stayed overnight at a country hotel, after attending her son's school concert at night. She was so delighted she cabled me in Australia from the hotel. Best of all, she can now work away from home, staying a full day on her own. She also goes to concerts, movies, and shops with her children, and when she remembers agoraphobia on these occasions, it is to think how once she could not do these things.

The following letter seems to have been written especially for those of you who are determined to come out of your illness by your own efforts:

Today's newspaper carried an article on phobias, and I was forcibly reminded of all the help Dr. Weekes's journals have brought me. I simply must write and say that my agoraphobia is almost a thing of the past. Even the trembling attacks that replaced it are no longer important.

As I strolled through the big stores yesterday, looking

at the midi skirts, I became aware of what I was doing and of how much I had improved. For one bittersweet moment I thought of all those wasted years when I was trapped. But there must be no looking back except in gratitude.

I feel Dr. Weekes's method has the same objective as the drug-relaxation method, which, although perhaps quicker, would not give the same basic understanding and permanent confidence as did her explanation and encouragement. The drug method is like going out and buying a bunch of flowers. Dr. Weekes's method means getting the seeds and growing the flowers yourself —much more rewarding.

I hope you will all persevere until the prize is yours. If you have the help of an understanding doctor, so much the better. If you have not, I assure you that however much you may have failed in the past, you can still do it on your own. This teaching is not only a cure for nervous illness but also a way of life; this too was said by a reader of these journals.

8

Coming through Setback

Since I have often mentioned setback in this book, some of the suggestions made previously must inevitably be repeated in this chapter. Coming through setback is such an important part of recovery, however, that it merits a section to itself and any necessary repetition.

IN A GOOD PERIOD THEY GATHER HOPE

Some people, on hearing a satisfactory explanation of their illness, lose fear of it and recover remarkably quickly. Others may frequently find themselves in a setback. Most nervously ill people are surprised to hear they can make as much progress toward recovery in a setback as in a good spell. In a good period they gather hope and feel the healing effect of peace, but often at the back of their mind lurks the thought that their illness may recur; and, of course, any remaining sensitization, helped by memory, will certainly do its best to see that "it" returns from time to time.

THE VERY SIGHT SPELLS WEARINESS

Memory is ready to waylay at every turn in the road. The sufferer has seen those houses, those streets, those shops, so often that the very sight spells weariness and illness. Each upsetting sensation that memory recalls may awaken such suffering that its victim can easily mistake memory for reality and think he has slipped to the bottom of the ladder once more. The contrast between the hope and peace experienced in a good spell and the suffering felt in a setback highlights the suffering and makes it seem more unendurable than ever.

This contrast makes the early setbacks seem especially severe and brings deep disappointment. It appears to the sufferer that whenever he tries to go forward, some "thing" is always ready to drag him back. He had thought that as he recovered, setbacks, if they occurred, would be less and less severe and would occur less frequently. And so they might, but the worst setback of all can come just before complete recovery. The nearness of recovery makes a setback at this time especially frustrating. And yet however severe setback may be, if it is coped with the right way, it does not retard ultimate recovery. Try to remember this.

YOU NEED NOT BE WAYLAID BY MEMORY

You should understand the tricks memory and habit can play so that you are not too discouraged by setback, however long it may last or whenever it may come. You should learn to appreciate the difference between memory and reality and know that when memory recalls past suffering and reawakens old sensations and apprehensions, *it is still only memory.* You need not be waylaid by memory, however painful and convincing it may seem.

Let memory recall as much as it may, but do not let this deceive you into thinking you have slipped into illness again, although for a while you may feel the symptoms as acutely as ever.

GRANDMA'S MUFFINS

When I was young, Grandma often had a batch of hot muffins waiting for me after school. When I smell hot muffins now, Grandma immediately comes to mind. I do not think, "Hot muffins! What do they remind me of? Ah, yes! Grandma!" I just automatically think of her.

Setback is like Grandma's muffins. Even when you are well, if something suddenly recalls your illness, you may feel the shadow of past suffering as quickly as I remember those muffins. When this happens, if you think, "Only Grandma's muffins!" you will help the shadow of the shadow to pass.

It is the unaccountable suddenness of setback that can shock, so that the sufferer seems temporarily at least to lose the power to reason with it and to quickly help himself. A woman wrote, "I have done well with desensitizing myself. I have a return of panic only about once a month now. It is strange, though: The further apart the spells come, the less I know how to handle them quickly. They come with a greater shock after a long peaceful period, and I'm so out of practice that for a while I forget your advice."

"MY EMOTIONS ARE WOBBLY WITH THE SHOCK OF SETBACK"

Another woman said:

When a setback strikes, it is sometimes quite a while before I can practice what you have taught me. The

setback seems so engulfing at first. It's difficult to make
my attitude positive quickly enough. My emotions are
so wobbly with the shock of setback that the encouragement I try to give myself doesn't get beyond words.
It doesn't register any feeling of belief or bring any
relief. I walk round all day giving myself words, words,
words. It takes quite a while before I can feel in
charge of the situation again. But this is gradually
getting better as I have more practice. I feel a little
more confident each time I find my way out of a setback, and I'm beginning to remember the way out more
readily.

ALL THE UPSETTING SYMPTOMS RETURN SO QUICKLY

One of the most shocking aspects of a setback can be the
quick return of *all* the upsetting symptoms. The sufferer
is tempted to think the number of returning symptoms is
a measure of the severity of the setback. It is not. If you
think of your cousin John, the chances are you will also
think of others in the family. This is no more than a chain
of related memories. All the symptoms of setback are the
symptoms of stress, of anxiety, so that their quick reappearance in full—as a family, as it were—simply means
you are very anxious again.

Just as the conductor of an orchestra can stop all
instruments with one rap of his baton, so you can calm
all symptoms with one treatment: acceptance. You do not
need a special lotion for your sweating hands, a special
tablet for giddiness and another for agitation. A mild
tranquilizer *and acceptance* work on all your symptoms,
so do not watch each symptom anxiously.

REACTIONS WITHOUT SO MUCH FEAR AND SHOCK

As understanding and acceptance heal sensitization,
feeling will not follow thought so swiftly or intensely,

and you will be able to reason less emotionally with your feelings, even less emotionally with panic. Confidence comes from experience, and some of your best experience lies in coming through setback because, as I said earlier, each setback gives yet another opportunity to practice until you make my teaching part of yourself, make it so built in that your reactions in any future disturbing situation will not be the old frightening flashback reactions but will gradually be the right ones—reactions without so much fear and shock. You will know the way out of setback so well that you will no longer fear the way in.

"Must I Always Have Setbacks?"

This answers the question so often asked, "Must I always have setbacks?" Setbacks gradually fade from the scene when you no longer fear them. You are completely cured when you no longer dread setback, because when you are no longer afraid of setback, it loses its meaning. It is no longer a set*back*; it becomes only a reminder of how you once suffered. Indeed, when you have learned to cope with a setback, it serves to highlight the progress you have made, and you can then look back on your illness with a sense of gratitude for having had the experience. Oh yes, this day will come, but it takes time. You must not count each day spent in a setback. You must not think, "Oh, my goodness. This one's lasted longer than any of the others! *This* will never go!"

If a setback is specially long, you will find it is because you are waiting too impatiently for it to go and are withdrawing from it in fear, you are impatiently trying to break your way through it, fight it, or you have become hopeless about recovering. *You must give as much time to coming through each setback as it demands.* Do not try to rush through, testing yourself each morning to see if you are feeling better. Do not watch yourself anxiously. You cannot step out of a setback like stepping out of a garment. Let it have its head; it will certainly take it anyhow, so you may as well give in gracefully and float with it.

WHEN YOU GO TO BED

Try not to despair when you go to bed at night because you are in a setback again. Understand that the more you worry about it, the more you resensitize yourself and the longer setback will remain. I know how tired you are of continually trying to get yourself "up off the floor." If you can do it without too much frustration, you will find peace all the sooner.

WELL ONE DAY, ILL THE NEXT

I am often asked why a nervously ill person can feel so well one day and then, for no apparent reason, so ill the next. For example, why can an agoraphobic person travel into town without fear one day and yet the next day feel the old fears as acutely as ever? Strangely enough, as stressed earlier, it is because yesterday's journey was so successful that he is vulnerable to defeat today. The memory of yesterday's success may make him overanxious to be just as successful again; so he may start the journey apprehensively—therefore slightly more sensitized than he was yesterday—with the result that it may take only some minor incident on the way into town to bring panic immediately. When this happens, he is convinced this journey will be a failure. So he despairs, and such acute emotion as despair sensitizes still further and makes him more vulnerable to the thought of failure. He is making the mistake of testing himself.

Remember, practice; never test. Do not set an examination for yourself to see if you can travel without panic

If you have panic after panic and yet try to take each the right way, the journey made with panic is just as successful as the journey made without it. Also, if you test yourself, failure brings a sense of defeat, whereas with practice, failure means only that you can practice again. Can you see the difference between testing and practicing? The very thought of testing brings tension, whereas the thought of practicing holds no urgent demand.

Also, doing the unusual, although it may be no more than boarding a bus, may seem very unreal, so that in the beginning, even when you are successful, there may be no feeling of achievement but only a feeling of strangeness. Indeed, your illness can seem more real than the early stages of recovery, and the journey into town—or any other undertaking—may have to be made successfully many times before it is accompanied by any sense of real achievement. Achievement must be consolidated before you can feel firm ground, an inner strength to face the future.

As I said earlier, when you understand the value of repeated achievement, achievement may become such an urgency that you may be afraid to let a day pass without practicing for fear you will lose what you have already gained. You will never lose what you have gained once you practice the right way. If physical illness brings a halt to your efforts, do not let postponement become a permanent avoidance.

Most Alarming of All Is the Return of Panic

When I review the difficulties of recovery, I would say the most alarming one of all is the return of panic weeks, even years, after recovery. In my experience, this unexpected reappearance of panic causes more concern than any other aspect of nervous illness. It shocks, it frightens, and *it reminds*. That is why it is so shocking. It reminds of so much one would rather forget forever, of so much one hoped one had forgotten forever.

The fear immediately added, together with the physical disturbance caused by panic, resensitizes slightly and helps bring back some of the old, perhaps almost forgotten, nervous sensations, so that the unwary sufferer may be bluffed into thinking "it" has returned or will return if he doesn't look out. Almost invariably he makes the old mistake of capitulating before the feeling and trying to run away from it.

One woman, after being well for a year, had a return of panic while shopping. She immediately dashed out of the shop and avoided it for weeks. She had once more retreated from fear, in fear.

Never do this. Never let an unexpected return of panic shock you into running away from it. Halt; go slowly. See the panic through, and then quietly go on with whatever you are doing. Let the panic come again and again if it wants to. Do not try to switch it off; do not withdraw blindly from it. Understand that some tension, some strain, may have slightly sensitized you once more or that memory, stirred by some sight, sound, thought, smell, may have flashed the old feeling. Any of us may at times become slightly sensitized by strain, so that we feel on edge, apprehensive. If this happens to one who has felt panic intensely in the past, his apprehension can quickly change to panic because the way to panic in him is so well worn. One could almost say his panic mechanism is well oiled and ready.

If you can accept that for a long time to come you may have a strong flash of panic from time to time, if you can realize that this means no more than that you are slightly sensitized for the moment or that memory has stirred the embers of your illness, and if you can see this panic through for what it is—only a physical feeling without real significance—then you are truly recovered despite occasional bouts of recurring panic. I remind you again that recovery from panic lies on the other side of panic, whenever it may come. Always see it through, and go on with the job at hand. Never run home in fear. Never begin avoiding again.

So:

- Accept everything about your illness.
- Do not waste energy trying to analyze every strange happening.
- Do not be dismayed by setback nor bluffed by memory.
- Do not despair when achievement seems unreal. Practice; never test.
- Do not be overawed by defeatist contemplation.
- Do not be dismayed if you feel nervier than ever when you first begin the journey to recovery.
- Do not be discouraged by physical illness.
- Above all, do not be shocked by returns of panic or by any strange flash experience.

You may think there is so much to remember, so much to do. There isn't, you know. It is all in one word: *accept*. Once you have the understanding this book brings, it will not matter if you forget the rest as long as you remember that one little word *accept*. Good luck.

Index